winning and managing
research funding

The Academic's Support Kit

Building your Academic Career
Rebecca Boden, Debbie Epstein and Jane Kenway

Getting Started on Research
Rebecca Boden, Jane Kenway and Debbie Epstein

Writing for Publication
Debbie Epstein, Jane Kenway and Rebecca Boden

Teaching and Supervision
Debbie Epstein, Rebecca Boden and Jane Kenway

Winning and Managing Research Funding
Jane Kenway, Rebecca Boden and Debbie Epstein

Building Networks
Jane Kenway, Debbie Epstein and Rebecca Boden

winning and managing

research funding

Jane **Kenway**

Rebecca **Boden**

Debbie **Epstein**

SAGE Publications
London • Thousand Oaks • New Delhi

SAGE Publications Ltd
1 Oliver's Yard
55 City Road
London EC1Y 1SP

SAGE Publications Inc.
2455 Teller Road
Thousand Oaks, California 91320

SAGE Publications India Pvt Ltd
B-42, Panchsheel Enclave
Post Box 4109
New Delhi 110 017

British Library Cataloguing in Publication data

A catalogue record for this book is available
from the British Library

ISBN 0 7619 4232 7 (Boxed set)

Library of Congress control number available

Typeset by C&M Digitals (P) Ltd, Chennai, India
Printed in Great Britain by Cromwell Press Ltd, Trowbridge, Wiltshire

Contents

Acknowledgements

Books such as these are, inevitably, the product of the labours, wisdom and expertise of a cast of actors that would rival that of a Hollywood epic.

Our biggest thanks go to our publishers, Sage, and especially Julia Hall and Jamilah Ahmed for unswerving enthusiastic support from the very beginning and for their careful and constructive advice throughout.

We would like to thank the authors of *Publishing in Refereed Academic Journals: A Pocket Guide* and especially Miranda Hughs for her hard work and insights which led the way conceptually.

Many people reviewed the initial proposal for the *Academic's Support Kit* at Sage's request and gave it a very supportive reception. We are grateful for their early faith in us and promise to use them as referees again!

The annotated Further Reading was excellently crafted by Penny Jane Burke, Geeta Lakshmi and Simon Robb. In addition, Elizabeth Bullen gave enormous help on issues of research funding and William Spurlin helped us unravel the complexities of US universities. All are valued friends and colleagues and we appreciate their efforts.

Much of the material in the *Kit* was 'road-tested' in sessions for our postgraduate students, colleagues and others. Many other people kindly gave their time to read and comment on drafts. We are very grateful to these human guinea pigs for their hard work and can assure our readers that, as far as we are aware, none of them was harmed in the experiment.

Chris Staff of the University of Malta devised the title the *Academic's Support Kit*, and he and Brenda Murphy provided glorious Mediterranean conditions in which to write. Malmesbury, Morwell and Gozo were splendid writing localities, although Dox 'added value' at Malmesbury with his soothing yet sonorous snoring.

We are grateful to our universities – Cardiff, Monash, South Australia and the West of England – for the material support and encouragement they gave the project.

Many people in many different universities around the world inspired the books and unwittingly provided the material for our vignettes. They are too many to mention by name and besides we have had to tell their stories under other names. We are deeply indebted to our colleagues, ex-colleagues, friends, enemies, students and past students, old lovers, past and present combatants and allies and all the managers that we have ever worked with for being such a rich source of illustration and inspiration!

We particularly thank that small and select band of people who have acted as a constant source of succour and support, wise guidance and true friendship at various crucial stages of our careers: Michael Apple, Richard Johnson, Diana Leonard, Alison Mackinnon, Fazal Rizvi, Gaby Weiner, Roger Williams and Sue Willis.

Finally, as ever, our greatest thanks go to our nearest and dearest, without whose tolerance, love and hard work these books would not be in your hands today.

J.K.
R.B.
D.E.

Introducing the *Academic's Support Kit*

Before you really get into this book, you might like to know a bit more about the authors.

Rebecca Boden, from England, is professor of accounting at the University of the West of England. She did her PhD in politics immediately after graduating from her first degree (which was in history and politics). She worked as a contract researcher in a university before the shortage of academic jobs in 1980s Britain forced her into the civil service as a tax inspector. She subsequently launched herself on to the unsuspecting world of business schools as an accounting academic.

Debbie Epstein, a South African, is a professor in the School of Social Sciences at Cardiff University. She did her first degree in history and then worked briefly as a research assistant on the philosopher Jeremy Bentham's papers. Unable to read his handwriting, she went on to teach children in a variety of schools for seventeen years. She returned to university to start her PhD in her forties and has been an academic ever since.

Jane Kenway, an Australian, is professor of education at Monash University with particular responsibility for developing the field of global cultural studies in education. She was a schoolteacher and outrageous hedonist before she became an academic. But since becoming an academic she has also become a workaholic, which has done wonders for her social life, because, fortunately, all her friends are similarly inclined. Nonetheless she is interested in helping next-generation academics to be differently pleasured with regard to their work and their lives.

As you can see, we have all had chequered careers which are far from the stereotype of the lifelong academic but that are actually fairly typical. What we have all had to do is to retread ourselves, acquire new skills and learn to cope in very different environments. In our current jobs we all spend a lot of time helping and supporting people who are learning to be or developing themselves as academics. Being an accountant, Rebecca felt that there had to be a much more efficient way of helping people to get the support they need than one-to-one conversations. This book and the other five in the *Academic's Support Kit* are for all these people, and for their mentors and advisers.

We have tried to write in an accessible and friendly style. The books contain the kind of advice that we have frequently proffered our research students and colleagues, often over a cup of coffee or a meal. We suggest that you consume their contents in a similar ambience: read the whole thing through in a relaxed way first and then dip into it where and when you feel the need.

Throughout the *ASK* books we tell the stories of anonymised individuals drawn from real life to illustrate how the particular points we are making might be experienced. While you may not see a precise picture of yourself, we hope that you will be able to identify things that you have in common with one or more of our characters to help you see how you might use the book.

Pragmatic principles/principled pragmatism

In writing these books, as in all our other work, we share a number of common perceptions and beliefs.

1. Globally, universities are reliant on public funding. Downward pressure on public expenditure means that universities' financial resources are tightly squeezed. Consequently mantras such as 'budgeting', 'cost cutting', 'accountability' and 'performance indicators' have become ubiquitous, powerful drivers of institutional behaviour and academic work.
2. As a result, universities are run as corporate enterprises selling education and research knowledge. They need 'management', which is essential to running a complex organisation such as a university, as distinct from 'managerialism' – the attempted application of 'scientific management techniques' borrowed from, though often discarded by, industry and commerce. What marks managerialism out from good management is the belief that there is a one-size-fits-all suite of management solutions that can be applied to any organisation. This can lead to a situation in which research and teaching, the *raison d'etre* of universities, take second place to managerialist fads, initiatives, strategic plans, performance

indicators and so on. Thus the management tail may wag the university dog, with the imperatives of managerialism conflicting with those of academics, who usually just want to research and teach well.

3. Increasingly, universities are divided into two cultures with conflicting sets of values. On the one hand there are managerialist doctrines; on the other are more traditional notions of education, scholarship and research. But these two cultures do not map neatly on to the two job groups of 'managers' and 'academics'. Many managers in universities hold educational and scholarly values dear and fight for them in and beyond their institutions. By the same token, some academics are thoroughly and unreservedly managerialist in their approach.

4. A bit like McDonald's, higher education is a global business. Like McDonald's branches, individual universities seem independent, but are surprisingly uniform in their structures, employment practices and management strategies. Academics are part of a globalised labour force and may move from country to (better paying) country.

5. Academics' intellectual recognition comes from their academic peers rather than their employing institutions. They are part of wider national and international peer networks distinct from their employing institutions and may have academic colleagues across continents as well as nearer home. The combination of the homogeneity of higher education and academics' own networks make it possible for them to develop local identities and survival strategies based on global alliances. The very fact of this globalisation makes it possible for us to write a *Kit* that is relevant to being an academic in many different countries, despite important local variations.

6. In order to thrive in a tough environment academics need a range of skills. Very often acquiring them is left to chance, made deliberately difficult or the subject of managerialist ideology. In this *Kit* our aim is to talk straight. We want to speak clearly about what some people just 'know', but others struggle to find out. Academia is a game with unwritten and written rules. We aim to write down the unwritten rules in order to help level an uneven playing field. The slope of the playing field favours 'developed' countries and, within these, more experienced academics in more prestigious institutions. Unsurprisingly, women and some ethnic groups often suffer marginalisation.

7. Most of the skills that academics need are common across social sciences and humanities. This reflects the standardisation of working practices that has accompanied the increasing managerialisation of universities, but also the growing (and welcome) tendency to work across old disciplinary divides. The *Academic's Support Kit* is meant for social scientists, those in the humanities and those in more applied or vocational fields such as education, health sciences, accounting, business and management.

8. We are all too aware that most academics have a constant feeling of either drowning in work or running ahead of a fire or both. Indeed, we often share these feelings. Nevertheless, we think that there *are* ways of being an academic that are potentially less stressful and more personally rewarding. Academics need to find ways of playing the game in ethical and professional ways and winning. We do not advise you to accept unreasonable demands supinely. Instead, we are looking for strategies that help people retain their integrity, the ability to produce knowledge and teach well.

9. University management teams are often concerned to avoid risk. This may lead to them taking over the whole notion of 'ethical behaviour' in teaching and research and subjecting it to their own rules, which are more to do with their worries than good professional academic practice. In writing these books, we have tried to emphasise that there are richer ethical and professional ways of being in the academic world: ways of being a public intellectual, accepting your responsibilities and applying those with colleagues, students and the wider community.

And finally …

We like the way that Colin Bundy, Principal of the School of Oriental and African Studies in London and previously Vice-Chancellor of the University of the Witwatersrand in Johannesburg, so pithily describes the differences and similarities between universities in such very different parts of the world. Interviewed for the *Times Higher Education Supplement* (27 January 2004) by John Crace, he explains:

> The difference is one of nuance. In South Africa, universities had become too much of an ivory tower and needed a reintroduction to the pressures

of the real world. In the UK, we have perhaps gone too far down the line of seeing universities as pit-stops for national economies. It's partly a response to thirty years of underfunding: universities have had to adopt the neo-utilitarian line of asserting their usefulness to justify more money. But we run the risk of losing sight of some of our other important functions. We should not just be a mirror to society, but a critical lens: we have a far more important role to play in democracy and the body politic than merely turning out graduates for the job market.

Our hope is that the *Academic's Support Kit* will help its readers develop the kind of approach exemplified by Bundy – playing in the real world but always in a principled manner.

Books in the *Academic's Support Kit*

The *Kit* comprises six books. There is no strict order in which they should be read, but this one is probably as good as any – except that you might read *Building your Academic Career* both first and last.

Building your Academic Career encourages you to take a proactive approach to getting what you want out of academic work whilst being a good colleague. We discuss the advantages and disadvantages of such a career, the routes in and the various elements that shape current academic working lives. In the second half of the book we deal in considerable detail with how to write a really good CV (résumé) and how best to approach securing an academic job or promotion.

Getting Started on Research is for people in the earlier stages of development as a researcher. In contrast to the many books available on techniques of data collection and analysis, this volume deals with the many other practical considerations around actually doing research – such as good ways to frame research questions, how to plan research projects effectively and how to undertake the various necessary tasks.

Writing for Publication deals with a number of generic issues around academic writing (including intellectual property rights) and then considers writing refereed journal articles, books and book chapters in detail as well as other, less common, forms of publication for academics. The aim is to demystify the process and to help you to become a confident, competent, successful and published writer.

Teaching and Supervision looks at issues you may face both in teaching undergraduates and in the supervision of graduate research students. This book is not a pedagogical instruction manual – there are plenty of those around, good and bad. Rather, the focus is on presenting explanations and possible strategies designed to make your teaching and supervision work less burdensome, more rewarding (for you and your students) and manageable.

Winning and Managing Research Funding explains how generic university research funding mechanisms work so that you will be better equipped to navigate your way through the financial maze associated with various funding sources. The pressure to win funding to do research is felt by nearly all academics worldwide. This book details strategies that you might adopt to get your research projects funded. It also explains how to manage your research projects once they are funded.

Building Networks addresses perhaps the most slippery of topics, but also one of the most fundamental. Despite the frequent isolation of academic work, it is done in the context of complex, multi-layered global, national, regional and local teaching or research networks. Having good networks is key to achieving what you want in academia. This book describes the kinds of networks that you might build across a range of settings, talks about the pros and cons and gives practical guidance on networking activities.

Who should Use this Book and Why?

This book is designed to help you win the money and other resources that you need to support your research and to assist you in using the lovely money once you have got it. Straitened research resources are, sadly, a global university phenomenon. And even though doing research is part of most people's job contract or at least expectations, most universities take the view that, to a substantial extent, academics must raise the money to do that work themselves. Nobody said it was a sane system.

Getting the funding to do our job can be a daunting prospect. Research funding systems are complex and vary considerably between disciplines, universities and countries. Nevertheless, there is some generic knowledge that, once acquired, will help you to navigate your own way.

There are many research websites and books (mentioned in Further Reading at the end of this book) that tell you how to write research proposals with a view to winning funding, and *Getting Started on Research* also gives you some strong pointers. We do not propose to replicate what they do here. Rather, we aim to help you understand university funding systems, locate possible funding sources, write winnable research applications and then manage the funds.

This book will be especially useful if you are in any of the following situations:

- You have some research experience and have seen through at least one research project. For instance, you may have a doctorate, have been a research assistant or an associate on someone else's project or have been a junior research partner in a research team. You now think that it is time to branch out and get your hands on some more substantial resources in order to pursue your work further.
- You may be employed in a 'contract research unit' in a university – a place where the payment of staff salaries is dependent upon winning external research funding. You might have been taken on in such a place as a junior research assistant and now want to establish your institutional position by winning your 'own' research monies.

- You may be a less experienced lecturer who has previously had small amounts of research support and funding from your university and are now wanting to or are coming under pressure to seek external funds.
- In terms of your career you may be just starting in the academic world, you may have been around for a while but mainly concentrating on your teaching and administration or you may be quite an experienced researcher but not experienced at winning external grants.
- You may be a mentor of any such people.

This is the point at which you may wish, or be pressured, to apply for external research funding. This is also the point at which you have to put your researcher identity on the line, as you are about to be subject to external scrutiny most probably in a highly competitive and/or a highly politicised funding environment. How do you feel? Possibly you feel quite vulnerable and exposed, possibly you feel stressed and stretched, and possibly you feel quite excited and challenged. Whatever the case, you know that there is a lot you do not know about this process and you are anxious to ascend a steep learning curve quickly and to produce winnable research applications as soon as possible. This book offers words of advice and caution.

Our first word of caution is *don't rush*. A hurried grant application is usually shoddy. Shoddy applications are highly unlikely to get funded and are bad for your reputation both with potential funders and indeed in your own university. Winning research grants is partly about your academic reputation: about developing a good one or about having a reputation for 'delivering quality outcomes' – as they say in polite management circles. If your bid is slapdash, assessors will assume that your research will be too. So take the time to prepare yourself to be a funded researcher and take time with your applications. Taking time at this stage may be frustrating in the short term but pays dividends, big time, in the long run.

You may:

- Feel completely in the dark about how this money thing works.
- Be unable to understand the key differences between the different sorts of support available and what the pros and cons of each are.
- Be bewildered by the array of possible sources and unsure about how to locate funding opportunities, or
- Need help in shaping yourself and your work to become a successful winner of research funds.

The positive incentives to apply for research funds are increasingly strong, whilst at the same time there are very real pressures on academics to 'perform' in this regard.

Let us now introduce you to some people who may be a bit like you. If not, other people you will meet throughout this book certainly will be.

George had been a teacher in a university for a number of years. He had been successful in getting some time allocated to him to start a small research project but then the dean vindictively decided that George's proper role was as a teacher and removed this resource from him. George enjoys his research and has therefore decided that he will seek external funding for it that will enable him to 'buy out' some of his teaching duties.

Louise has recently completed her PhD. During her examination for this, one of the examiners suggested that she should take one particular aspect of her work and develop it further – something she had not been able to pursue in the PhD itself. Louise is anxious to do this but she has recently been appointed as a lecturer and is struggling to cope with her new job. Some research funding would enable her to maintain her research momentum and also relieve her of some of the more tedious aspects of her teaching work. It would also impress her new bosses if she could win external funding.

Mohammed has been a successful researcher for a number of years, has been steadily promoted as a result and is now quite senior. He has reached a position where his university is pressing him to apply for external funding – something he has never really bothered with before. Whilst a confident and competent researcher, he is unsure about how to go about it and feels that he would look foolish if he asked someone.

The Research Funding Pressure Cooker

In this chapter we explain what we mean by 'research funding', introduce you to some key concepts you will need to know, describe your likely position within funding systems and give you some pointers as to how to understand the contexts within which you may have to operate.

What do you mean, 'research funding'?

All research requires heaps of resources: your time, machinery (such as computers), books, libraries, travel, conference fees and so on. All these have to be paid for. For those academics in the arts, humanities and the social sciences, the biggest single cost is likely to be time – someone has to pay your salary and those of research assistants, librarians and other staff.

If you are employed within a university, where does the money come from? Very broadly, there are two main sources of money to support research activities.

- *Money that flows to the academic institution (unrestricted funds)*. This is the money that universities and other higher education institutions get as institutions. It can take many forms: it may be 'core funding' from state and/or national government, income from trust funds or endowments, bequests from grateful ex-students, income from the sale of university assets such as land or rare books in the library, the profits on university trading activities such as publishing, catering or facilitating conferences, royalties on patents based on staff work and so on. The exact mix of this money at your university will depend on the country you are in and the nature of your institution.

- In countries such as the UK, Australia and South Africa most of this income will be core funding from government. Increasingly, governments tend to support higher education because they think it is an important activity that underpins economic competitiveness. The precise way in which governments calculate how much to give higher education institutions will vary between states and countries. Because funding mechanisms can be a really useful way of influencing institutional actions, governments and other organisations that give core funding tend to set up systems of allocation that support the objectives of the giver. For instance, if a government wants to increase the number of young people going to university, it may make taking extra students a financially attractive proposition for universities. However, generally, once the university has been given these funds, it can spend them on whatever it pleases – for instance, it might receive extra money for taking extra students but just have larger class sizes and spend the additional income on research. It might be helpful to think of such money as *unrestricted university funds* – no restrictions are placed on the university as to how it is spent.

Because universities are generally independent, self-governing institutions, when all this type of money comes in the university itself generally has discretion over how it is used. So a university committed to increasing its research profile might decide to channel an increased amount of income into funding research activities. It might choose to deploy the money in a number of ways – for instance, lightening the teaching load of academic staff so that they can get on with research, or making funds available for conferences. But remember that, just as funding is a useful means by which external funders such as governments influence universities, the same is true between universities and individual members of staff. Whilst some universities may distribute such resources evenly across all staff and let them get on with it, others may make the allocation of resources the subject of a competition among staff. Some will operate a mixture of these two systems – for instance, everyone might get the same teaching relief but staff would have to get a paper accepted for a conference in order to secure funding to go to it.

- *Money that flows to universities for specific purposes (restricted funds).* This is the money (and sometimes other resources such as time on a big machine like a telescope) that external funders allocate not to the unrestricted funds of the university but rather for a specific, defined piece of research work. That work might be an individual project, to run a research centre or to fund a conference. A variety of external agencies provide such funds. The funders here might include government, charitable foundations or organisations in the private or not-for-profit sectors. The funders' motives may be altruistic or they may want some piece of knowledge the better to further their profit-seeking objectives (and sometimes the two shade together).

The important thing to remember here is that such money can be used only for the precise purposes for which it is given. Such funds might usefully be thought of as *restricted funds* – because their application can be quite tightly controlled. Such restricted funds are an even more precise means of controlling universities and their research agendas than the mechanisms for calculating the allocation of unrestricted funds. 'We'll fund project *x* on subject *y*, but not project *a* on subject *b*.' This type of restricted funding is becoming increasingly popular with governments, as it gives them a great way to directly influence the research agenda. In countries such as Australia and the UK, and probably others, governments are increasingly channelling funding through the restricted rather than the unrestricted route.

The distinction between the two types of money, like all accounting, is not always precise or objective. For instance, *restricted* funding may include elements of so-called 'overhead costs' – contributions to general university costs that may be siphoned away into university unrestricted funds and spent, for instance, as 'seed corn funding' for further research projects. Alternatively, because bidding for restricted funds can be viciously competitive on price, universities may offer cut-price deals to external funding agencies, subsidising such work from their unrestricted funds.

Whilst money is a useful means of controlling things like research agendas, it is important to realise that this does not mean that you have to be buffeted around on the capricious winds of those who fund research, be it your own university or external agencies like government. You may, however, have to 'package' your work in particular ways, put a 'spin' on it or otherwise do the 'hard sell' in order to secure the access to resources that you need. In order to do this, you need to learn about, analyse and understand your own local funding environment.

Some basic concepts

As will be clear from the section above, there are many different sorts of 'research' money available. The language people use varies considerably between universities, systems and countries. Here is a glossary of some of the more common terms. We use these terms in this way in this book. However, you need to know how the terms are used in your own situation.

Research. The fundamental notion here is that research is about the generation of new knowledge or new applications of knowledge. For instance, in financial economics, the development of new knowledge might include the formulation of new mathematical models of how stock markets work. Research that applies such understandings might include an analysis of how a particular stock market has functioned in certain circumstances. The distinction often drawn here is between *basic* or *pure* research and *applied* research. Despite the best efforts of many people over many years, it remains a fact that it is almost impossible to draw sharp distinctions between these different gradations of research activity. Another distinction sometimes employed is between *strategic* research and *contract* research. The former applies to research where the research topic and questions pursued are identified by the researchers themselves. In contradistinction, the term *contract* research is used where the research topics, questions, etc., are developed by the organisation funding the research.

Consultancy. We would define consultancy as the process through which you provide paying customers with the benefit of your expertise and knowledge in order to provide answers to specific problems that they have identified. The difference between consultancy and contract research is difficult to define. For instance, a social policy researcher may be contracted by the Social Security Ministry in her country to research the reasons why potential welfare recipients fail to apply for the payments that they are entitled to. She might then be hired as a consultant by the same Ministry to translate her knowledge of such issues into practical solutions to the Ministry's problems of low welfare take-up.

Evaluation. Evaluations involve an assessment of the merits or otherwise of an existing situation, programme or policy perhaps according to the criteria laid down for the establishment of such. These can be either formative (as they develop and are put into practice) or summative (once they are complete or have gone through a certain round). For instance, to return to the social policy research/consultant above, she may subsequently be asked to conduct an evaluation of the Ministry's procedures, processes and performance with regard to getting potential welfare recipients to apply for their benefits.

Research (of whatever variety), *consultancy* and *evaluation* all shade into each other in what can be quite confusing ways and involve interesting status hierarchies among academics. But the matter doesn't stop there for your university – these status hierarchies can also impact on the funding of universities. For instance, in Australia and the UK universities are financially rewarded by government for attracting *research* money, but not for earning *consultancy* income. For this reason, *consultancy* income is often subject to the creative accountant's version of semantics and reclassified as *contract research*. At the same time, universities can also be anxious to demonstrate that they have *consultancy* income, as this enables them to argue that they are assisting the economic development of the country and producing 'relevant' and 'useful' knowledge.

It is important to note that, although consultancy and evaluation work can be an essential part of 'performing' your role as an academic (see *Building an Academic Career*), it is not research work *per se*. That said, such work can and does successfully facilitate aligned research work – for instance by providing funding to look at problems, access to data or people and so on.

Why should I be interested in all this?

Because research requires resources, you will need access to these in order to do it. The amount of money people need to do research varies markedly according to discipline, topic, time-lines and personal preference. When thinking about the resources that you need and have available for research it can be helpful to categorise it in two ways.

- *Mode I support.* This is financial and other resource support that you may get as of right in your university. For instance, you may be in a position where all academic staff are given a certain amount of time during their working week to conduct research in, or have an entitlement to go to, say, one international conference a year. Alternatively, you might think of the cost of the provision of a good library as part of this type of research support. This type of support usually comes from universities' *unrestricted funds*.

- *Mode II support.* This is where you have to actively go out and seek the financial and other resources for your work. This may well be competitive with other researchers within or outside your university. For instance, you may have to apply to your organisation for study leave, presenting a cogent and convincing case. Alternatively, you might apply to an external funding body for cash to buy you out of all teaching for a year while you conduct a specific research project. This type of support may come from either the university's *unrestricted funds* (and the organisation has decided to have a competition for its allocation) or constitute *restricted funds*. Either way, you will have had to be proactive in making moves to get the cash.

In our experience, support is becoming very tightly squeezed as a result of the general squeeze on *unrestricted* funding that we discussed above. In some disciplines, at some universities and in some job contracts it is entirely possible to do the work that you want to do on Mode I support. In fact, some very productive and influential researchers in philosophy or literature, say, never actively seek funding at all. Their Mode I support gives them all the time that they need to read, think and write and to systematically rummage around in the library, on the Web or in various archives.

Mode I research support has a number of advantages:

- Arts, social science and humanities research can often be done on very little money, saving the researcher the considerable time and effort involved in winning Mode II support.
- You can choose your own foci and work to your own time-lines.
- You don't have to worry about the priorities and preferences and 'deliverable' deadlines of funding agencies.
- Your work may be of the type where it is difficult to attract any other sort of support, but be no less valuable for that.
- This type of support can be used strategically to do small, pilot projects, and publish from them, to improve your chances of getting research funding.

Lucia is now a senior scholar in the field of leadership. But at one stage early in her career she was frustrated by the difficulties she was experiencing in attracting funding to undertake research she wanted to conduct on women in leadership. A more senior colleague encouraged her to undertake a small pilot project using Mode I support to provide the basis for a funded project grant application. She then selected a small and interesting group of women leaders, interviewed them and from the interviews identified the core questions and issues for a later successful funding bid.

The down side of using Mode I support is that the pressure is still on you to bring in money. This is often because universities are anxious to get their hands on the 'overhead costs' that we mentioned above. And, depending on which field you are in and on the way that your university thinks about the matter, you may be seen as less valuable as a researcher in comparison with others who do bring in money. This, sadly, may be the case even if you are putting out well recognised and reviewed publications. Indeed, you may find you are not as popular with your head of school as you would like to be and that your teaching load is increased to free up others to do externally funded research. Further, you may proceed for several years without any significant experience of writing applications and winning such funds. Then, if you do begin to chase money, you will probably find you do not have the necessary grant-writing skills.

Giovanni is an experienced academic and has produced some remarkable papers. She has relied on small amounts of Mode I support and some internally provided Mode II money to support her research and has usually secured such money without much difficulty. However, when preference for internal money was given to early career researchers she was at a disadvantage. She was forced to compete for the money she needed in wider and more competitive research circles. Her early endeavours in such circles were marred by her lack of experience in bidding for external money and by her limited knowledge of the tricks of the trade. Having her first external grant application rejected led her to seek some help and to do some fast 'upskilling'.

In short, it is unwise to rely exclusively on Mode I support. The rest of this book deals with the thorny question of how to win and manage Mode II money. Although social scientists, arts and humanities researchers don't usually seek or receive as much money as those in the so-called hard sciences, they can and do attract the big bucks. There are no hard-and-fast rules about the amount of money that you should seek.

There are many reasons why you should try to secure Mode II research funding:

- It may enable you to broaden and deepen your research work in a way that enhances your field, discipline and indeed your subsequent academic career.
- It may free you of some of the more burdensome and tedious aspects of your university work, enabling you to concentrate more intensely on the work you really love.
- In some environments, it may be the only means of actually finding support for your research.
- This is the direction in which university researchers are being pushed as part of the 'performance culture' that now permeates most institutions.
- It wins you prestige within and beyond your university, a degree of bargaining capacity and academic independence.
- It looks good on your CV and assists your promotion and employment chances.

At the most pragmatic level, you can use your research money to:

- Employ research assistants (e.g. for literature reviews, gathering and interpreting data, setting up field visits, archival work, filing, editing and so much more – but you cannot use it for babysitting or shopping).
- Buy equipment.
- Buy out some of your teaching and marking.
- Host visiting scholars.
- Conduct conferences, seminars and workshops.
- Travel to: research sites including archive sites, consult with colleagues and conferences and network opportunities.
- Develop research centres or institutes.

Funding may well allow you to do research you otherwise could not do because of other commitments. Here is an example of one source of funds for this sort of activity. ('Science' in this context includes social science.)

The European Science Foundation (ESF) Exploratory Workshops allow leading European scientists to meet to explore novel ideas at the European level.

The aim of a workshop is to:

- initiate the exchange of knowledge and experiences between researchers from across Europe in an emerging area of research;
- help establish new collaborative links between different disciplines;
- test innovative ideas and develop potential collaborative research projects.

Each year the ESF Scientific Standing Committees select particular topics of interest as well as providing the opportunity for an 'open' section.

Applications must demonstrate the potential importance of European collaboration in the chosen field (European added value).

(Follow the Exploratory Workshop link from http://www.esf.org/, accessed 23 January 2004)

Mode II money may support:

- Discrete projects.
- Seminars and conferences.
- Research centres.
- National and international research networks.
- Major equipment/software purchases.

If you approach such support strategically then you can ensure outputs that can lead to future funding and other benefits such as building research networks. Mode II support may be valuably underpinned by Mode I support from your university that may involve, for instance, the provision of the services of support staff. This is often known as 'in kind' support and is invaluable.

Shirley and Alison both held postdoctoral positions at an Australian university and both had an interest in aging and in innovative research methodologies for researching it. Encouraged by their research centre director, they gained 'in kind' support to run a mini-conference on 'researching aging'. They invited established and new researchers to write papers discussing the research methodologies they employ to undertake their research. These papers were circulated beforehand and then 'workshopped' at a day-long mini-conference. The papers were then revised for an edited book. This whole process allowed Shirley and Alison not only to address their shared research interests, to gain experience at running a conference and editing a book but also to provide leadership in their field by bringing an inventive set of papers together into a book. They also provided one of the building blocks of their subsequent research careers.

In summary, you might find it helpful to think of research funding money as the fuel that drives university research. You can classify how this fuel is delivered and used as a 2×2 matrix – restricted/unrestricted funds promoting Mode I/Mode II research. In Figure 1, we've represented this matrix as a four-chamber research combustion engine, indicating the availability of and horsepower generated by the different types of fuel and activities. As you will see, it's not going to be a terribly smooth-running engine because, unlike a sweet engine, it can't fire equally well on all four cylinders.

What are the contexts of funding?

There are several contexts you need to understand in order to maximise your chances of attracting research funding and, yes, it's hot inside. This is partly because research funding is inevitably caught up in the wider politics of knowledge production, circulation and consumption. There is no escaping this, and one of your responsibilities as a researcher is to develop an understanding of such wider politics, not just as they apply to you but also as they apply to funding agencies and publishers, the research community as a whole and to various disciplines and sectors within it. An understanding of the politics will help to make you an astute bidder for funds but it will also alert you to at least some of the ethical issues associated with particular funding opportunities.

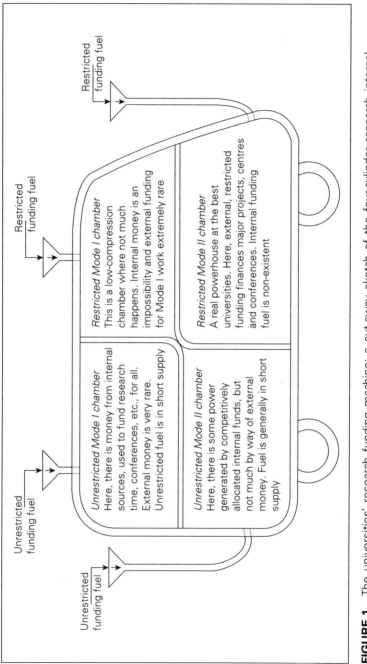

Unrestricted Mode I chamber
Here, there is money from internal sources, used to fund research time, conferences, etc., for all. External money is very rare. Unrestricted fuel is in short supply

Unrestricted Mode II chamber
Here, there is some power generated by competitively allocated internal funds, but not much by way of external money. Fuel is generally in short supply

Restricted Mode I chamber
This is a low-compression chamber where not much happens. Internal money is an impossibility and external funding for Mode I work extremely rare

Restricted Mode II chamber
A real powerhouse at the best universities. Here, external, restricted funding finances major projects, centres and conferences. Internal funding fuel is non-existent

Unrestricted funding fuel

Unrestricted funding fuel

Restricted funding fuel

Restricted funding fuel

FIGURE 1 The universities' research funding machine: a cut-away sketch of the four-cylinder research internal combustion engine

Your own university

The first context you need to be savvy about is your own university. This is for two reasons. First, you might want access to some of the university's jealously guarded unrestricted funds and, second, if you want to apply to an external funder then you will have to do so *through* the university. (This is because the contract relating to the eventual funds will be between the funder and the university, not you.)

Each university has increasingly elaborate structures and processes internal to it that relate to research and research grants. You need to familiarise yourself with these within your own school or department and within other layers of the university more widely. You should locate a chart that lays out the structures and the individual roles (e.g. dean of research, pro-vice-chancellor of research and so on), the committees and the responsibilities associated with them and the administrative structures and personnel. You should seek out the key people involved in research leadership and administration and get to know them and have them get to know your research foci and achievements. Try to get some insider knowledge – in some cases this may involve getting on some key committees.

You will need to find out information that will help you seek funds and will clarify what you are required to do when submitting an application. These may include the following:

- Sources of research support, information, assistance and advice – especially about budgets and about how much money you will be expected to charge for university infrastructure and the like (see further below). Universities also have lawyers and business or financial managers or budget officers who can help you with budget contracts.
- Sources of seed funding.
- Information about available external grants and time-lines. This will usually include the time-lines for you to submit certain bids through the university and its subsystems. University research officers are the people to talk to here, and they are usually 'worth their weight in gold'.
- Information about the processes that you must go through to get each grant 'signed off' by your head of school perhaps or dean. Most universities have policies you must follow and these are usually on their websites.
- Information about research reporting procedures.
- Chairs or members of ethics committees can advise you about the ethics processes associated with your projects.

Below is an example of the sort of thing we are talking about when we mention administrative support. Check out your own university's website and you will find something similar, along with a whole swath of material about pertinent people, policies and procedures – the vital three Ps.

University of British Columbia: Office of Research Services Overview

The ORS is responsible for the following research administration functions:

- Providing information and assistance in the research grant application process.
- Providing the institutional signature for research grant applications.
- Establishing research accounts and spending limits for research grants in accordance with UBC and granting agency policies.
- Providing administrative support for a variety of research programs offered by several internal UBC committees.
- Ensuring compliance with government regulations and granting agency requirements for the use of human subjects, animal subjects and biohazardous materials in research conducted at UBC.
- Establishing inter-institutional arrangements for the transfer of funds to research collaborators at other institutions.
- Providing statistical information on research funding at UBC.

(http://www.orsil.ubc.ca/overview.htm, accessed 23 January 2004)

You should also know that the university carefully monitors your research performance, and that winning grants is understood as part of that performance. So next to your name on lists at various levels of the organisation will be a record of the research grants you have won, the title, the amount of money and the funding body. You are under surveillance, like it or not. One sure way to accrue Brownie points with those further up the food chain in your university is to bring in research money – especially if the amounts are substantial, come from prestigious sources, and/or if you miraculously manage to generate a surplus which can be raked off by the university. The capacity to attract research income has become more and more important to universities because of wider changes in the university sector. And it is helpful for you to know about these changes so that you can understand the pressures on your university and by extension on you – and consider how best to deal with them.

The university sector: a national focus

Universities worldwide tend to be short of cash, and this is particularly the case in the UK, Australia, New Zealand and Canada, where unrestricted funds from public sources have seriously diminished. It is not so much the case in certain parts of Europe where the flow of unrestricted funds to universities is still quite strong or in the USA, where there are many independently wealthy universities. Added to this, governments are increasingly shifting the funds they do give from the *unrestricted* category to the *restricted*. This means that there is less money overall, a decline in large 'block grants' and greater competition for and control over the expenditure of available funds.

In turn, universities now expect the researchers that they employ to apply for Mode II funds. This cash helps universities to get research done (thereby enhancing their profile and legitimating their mission statements). It also provides much-needed 'overhead' monies – those elements of such funding that are paid to cover the universities' more or less fixed costs such as keeping the buildings warm or cool and maintaining the library. Moreover, winning external funding – especially that which leads to prestigious publications – may bring bonuses from government in terms of *unrestricted funds*. For instance, in the regular UK Research Assessment Exercise, the quantum measures of research performance include external research funding won. The better the department's overall score, the more money the government gives individual universities in *unrestricted funds*. Overall, what this system of bonuses means is that if universities are to undertake their 'core business' of research, staff must attract research funds. If they do not, the university loses its identity as a 'real' university and loses status within the university 'league table' system, and staff at that university have their opportunities to do research reduced. It's a vicious circle. What's more, it's important to note that just because your university receives overheads or additional unrestricted funds as a result of your successful research funding bids, it doesn't mean that you will necessarily benefit directly. The money is most likely to be spirited away for use or distribution by university research managers – or at best shared between you and them.

Because governments are now not only making less cash available but also expect universities to align themselves more closely with 'customers' for their research output, researchers are encouraged to seek funding not only from the public sector but also from all other sources (discussed later). This is usually referred to as 'diversifying the research funding base'. It is increasingly the case that, at the behest of their university, researchers are looking further afield for research money and at sources that they once might not have considered. They are expected to be highly lateral in their thinking in this regard.

This is clearly a game not of your own choosing but you can learn to play the game and to consider ways of winning without losing your ideals – at least, not all of them. Keep in mind that while managers do have to focus on income streams and thus want you to generate income to help the institution to stay afloat financially, they also have an interest in research reputations and in the identity of the university as a research-intensive institution. They want to bask in your reflected glory. Your aims are somewhat different – to generate funding to support your research and, indirectly, that of your colleagues.

Universities – a global/regional/international focus

Of course, many universities now understand themselves as global institutions and have links with international, supranational or transnational institutions that provide research funding. In other words, the nation state and those within it are no longer seen as the only source of research funding. Equally, as universities 'partner' in one way or another with universities across national borders, and as researchers become better linked with their international colleagues through email, the Web and increased travel for teaching and research purposes, new opportunities for research funding and research teams arise. So, too, do new research foci. If, for instance, you are one of those people involved in international teaching, you are well placed to spot new research and funding possibilities. Equally, all researchers should now keep their eyes peeled for new funding opportunities outside their own country, and, as time goes on, these funding opportunities will both increase and also become more competitive. We discuss examples of cross-border research funding possibilities below.

In sum, you will inevitably have to face the prospect of applying for research funding of some sort at some time in your career. In the main, unrestricted, internal funding is likely to be increasingly constrained. This means that you will have to look increasingly at sources of funding external to your university. In the next chapter we introduce you to these types of funders, and then go into some detail about how to access specific information on them.

3   Getting to Know the Funding Agencies

In this chapter we introduce you to the generic forms of external funding agencies – and describe their general characteristics.

What are the main sources of funding?

Generally speaking, funds will be available from the following types of sources, which we elaborate on later:

- Your own university.
- Government research funding organisations. The job of these organisations is to allocate government funds for research.
- Government contract research (for Ministries and agencies). Here, as distinct from government research-funding organisations, government departments or agencies may specifically contract researchers to undertake research of a more consultancy type.
- Foundations and charitable trusts. These may have as their main focus the sponsorship of research or they may combine this with other sorts of activity, such as philanthropic work.
- Private sector corporations. These organisations may need research/consultancy work undertaken to help them with specific work they are trying to do. For instance, a private company manufacturing mobile phones may need to know the best way of marketing them and may employ a social anthropologist to advise it on the role of mobile phone technology in youth culture.

In this globalised age there are also a number of organisations that provide funding for research which is not confined within nation states – hereafter referred to as 'states'. The terms employed here are 'international', 'supranational' and 'transnational' organisations. These are contested terms. We are using them in the following ways:

- *International organisations* are those which include national representatives who remain accountable to their home state.
- *Supranational organisations* are those which exist above nations, have members from many states but are accountable only to themselves.
- *Transnational organisations* may be based in one country but operate in many and are not aligned with any particular state. These are usually global corporations.

While these may be formal definitions, they don't give an adequate indication of the relationships of power that exist between states and these different organizations.

What do funding bodies tend to have in common?

Many funders have:

- Funding rounds at certain times of the year.
- Restrictions on which individuals and organisations can apply (e.g. some organisations reserve some funds for 'young scholars' or 'emerging researchers').
- Very explicit application processes and reject, out of hand, applications that do not conform exactly.
- Nominated areas of focus or priority.
- Information on the maximum amount of funding available per project but will also indicate the average amount allocated and explain that getting the maximum is rare.
- Limits on the number of grants you can hold simultaneously.
- The expectation that they will be persuaded of the significance of your project and its impact or benefit.
- Increased their emphasis on partnerships across the public/private divide and across nations.
- Become very positively disposed to collaborative links between different disciplines and to the development of collaborative research projects.
- An emphasis on innovation. (Sometimes they will even explain what they mean by this term.)
- Their assessment criteria laid out in the information and guidelines to applicants that they provide.
- A range of research they are prepared to fund which may be so broad as to include research centres – but usually not.

Some also:

- Ask for short (perhaps two-page) expressions of interest in the first instance and usually require the following information: name; organisation; concise statement of the purpose, justification and cost of the project; other sources of funds and contributions; and referees.
- Have established links with particular individuals, teams or universities and prefer to work with them. Consequently it may be difficult – and certainly very time-consuming – to build new links with them.
- Expect 'co-financing' or matching funds or at least some contribution in kind from the applicants and their organisation: if these can be 'leveraged' then the grant is looked upon more favourably. This is also called 'co-funding from alternative sources', which include industry, trusts, foundations and various national sources and international sources.
- Specify 'deliverables' over the duration of the grant as well as at the end.
- Are very keen on such key words as 'multi-stakeholder collaboration', 'capacity building', 'knowledge dissemination' and 'synergies'.

What are the key differences between funding agencies?

Funding agencies differ in lots of ways that will become evident as we proceed, but two of the main differences you need to be aware of are the sort of research they fund and their attitude to knowledge. Some include in their funding programmes research that is directed to the production and dissemination of new knowledge – basic or what is sometimes also called curiosity-driven research. Here knowledge does not necessarily have to have an immediate utility. Others place much more emphasis on research likely to have an immediate impact and which has an action and change orientation. As indicated earlier, this is called applied research or sometimes called policy-relevant research. Clearly, the distinctions are not always easy to uphold and are a matter of considerable debate in research circles.

The other key difference to note is who initiates the focus of the research – the researcher or the funding body. This has many implications for the power you have over the research and its outcomes and outputs – so to speak.

Who are the funders?

At the beginning of this chapter we identified the various major types of potential funding body. Most funding bodies have their own websites at which the details of their funding programmes are identified. Obviously it is up to you to chase up various organisations and find out what they say on their websites. We provide details from some websites as illustrative examples only and clearly things may have changed since the times we accessed the sites.

Your own university

Whilst money from your own institution is not external, we mention it here for important reasons. Often internal university grants provide you with a research launch pad. Through internal money you can get funded for small-scale projects from which to begin to publish and establish your research profile and reputation. Such funding can also give you a much-needed apprenticeship in learning how to manage a funded research project. It is a good idea to apply for these early and to make the most of them in terms of outcomes and outputs. Some universities give priority for internal funding to early career research researchers in order to give them a 'leg up'. However, in the longer term it is sensible not to rely on internal university money, and the more senior you get the more you will be expected to seek outside funds.

As we noted earlier, you can win internal university money for a range of research-related activities. Take a further example. Some universities provide support for research groups or research centres. You may be in the position to form such a group or at least to join one. Such groupings are beneficial for the following reasons. They:

- Usually provide administrative or research assistance support for members.
- Concentrate the efforts of like-minded researchers to produce what is called a 'critical mass' of people who work together and develop a collective sensibility and reputation.
- Provide you with immediate opportunities for team research and research-related activities such as inviting visiting scholars and running reading groups.
- Often include experienced and emerging researchers and thus mean you have ready access to potential mentors.

Government research-funding organisations

There are two main sources of research funds from governments. The differences between them are considerable and it is important to understand this. Most governments have organisations usually called something like 'research councils'. These are the traditional funders of basic and applied university research, acting as a conduit for funds between government and researchers. The second source, which we deal with below, is where government contracts university researchers for a specific piece of consultancy-type research.

Research councils are organised into fields of research and this varies across countries. For instance, in the UK there are a number of research councils. Those that are most relevant to readers of this book are the Economic and Social Research Council and the Arts and Humanities Research Board. The National Research Foundation is the South African government's national agency promoting basic and applied research and innovation across a wide range of fields. In Canada there are also a number of research councils; the most relevant for readers of this book is likely to be the Social Sciences and Humanities Research Council of Canada. You should also note that a number of other research councils which, from their names, may not seem relevant to you may also be worth exploring – for instance, the Engineering and Physical Sciences Research Council in the UK does fund a small amount of social science and business research. The following are examples from other countries.

Research agencies in various countries

- Commonwealth Department of Education, Science and Training Co-operative Research Centres (Australia)
- Australian Research Council
- Centre national de la recherche scientifique/National Centre for Scientific Research (France)
- Bundesministerium für Bildung, Wissenschaft, Forschung und Technologie/Federal Ministry of Education, Science, Research and Technology (Germany)
- Deutsche Forschungsgemeinschaft/German Research Foundation (Germany)

▶

▶
- Israel Science Foundation (Israel)
- Consiglio Nazionale delle Ricerche/National Research Council (Italy)
- Ministry of Education, Culture, Sports, Science and Technology (Japan)

Most research councils have comprehensive websites that give details of such things as:

- Thematic priorities (that is, the broad areas that the council sees as being priorities).
- 'End users' (a term used to describe those who, at the end of the day, will use research findings).
- Application processes and information for award holders.
- Peer review and decision making.
- Reporting and evaluation.
- Frequently asked questions.
- Links to other sites that may be of use.

Some also give you information about past grant winners and patterns of funding, and this helps you to see where you fit in this scenario.

The grants provided by research councils are highly competitive and prestigious. Winning them is great for your sense of self as a researcher and also for your reputation. However, just as they involve high expectations, so they also entail heavy responsibilities. You must deliver on what you say you will – of course, that is the case with all research grants. Research councils expect full reports and these all go on record and may be accessed when you apply for further funding.

National governments are increasingly sensitive to the benefits of research that has an international sensibility and, through their research councils, are encouraging researchers to consider the international aspects of their research questions. In addition, some are keen to support research that involves international research partnerships of various sorts. The following example from the ESRC in the UK illustrates the point and indicates some of the strategies employed to achieve this end.

ESRC international policy and strategy

Vision

The scope of the social sciences is international. They transcend national boundaries and nation states in their methods and subjects of enquiry, and in the knowledge, which they produce. The ESRC's role in developing social science in the UK involves a strong commitment to work across national boundaries, taking advantage of the intellectual opportunities to be gained from co-operative and comparative research as well as maintaining and developing the high standing of UK researchers within international social science research networks. Council's international commitment is embedded in its strategic goals. In particular, Council endorses the aspirations of the European Research Area in addressing the fragmentation of much European research with a view to increasing European competitiveness and enhancing the evidence base that contributes to the design of policy in response to common problems facing European societies. Council's commitment to strengthening its role as a national and an international player will enable it to gain maximum benefit for the social science community from new opportunities for research funding and co-operation as they develop. It will also ensure that the research undertaken is of maximum benefit to users.

Strategy

The strengthening of the Council's international commitment requires:

- Changes in the Council's strategic planning priorities.
- Mainstreaming the international research agenda as a generic concern for all Council Boards and Committees.
- Adapting the allocations of financial resources by the Boards and the allocation of time and staff resources within the Council's offices.

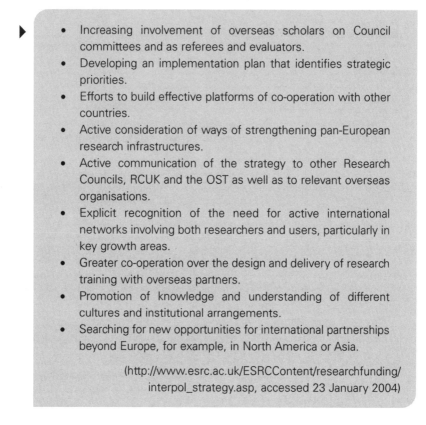

- Increasing involvement of overseas scholars on Council committees and as referees and evaluators.
- Developing an implementation plan that identifies strategic priorities.
- Efforts to build effective platforms of co-operation with other countries.
- Active consideration of ways of strengthening pan-European research infrastructures.
- Active communication of the strategy to other Research Councils, RCUK and the OST as well as to relevant overseas organisations.
- Explicit recognition of the need for active international networks involving both researchers and users, particularly in key growth areas.
- Greater co-operation over the design and delivery of research training with overseas partners.
- Promotion of knowledge and understanding of different cultures and institutional arrangements.
- Searching for new opportunities for international partnerships beyond Europe, for example, in North America or Asia.

(http://www.esrc.ac.uk/ESRCContent/researchfunding/
interpol_strategy.asp, accessed 23 January 2004)

The strategies listed indicate a serious process of gearing up for an expansion of international research, so this is clearly a matter to keep in mind as you develop your research agenda and networks; as predictably, support for international research will only increase.

Further, within nations there are funding bodies that fund international research, i.e. they fund people to go outside their own countries to conduct research in others. An example is the International Research and Exchanges Board (IREX):

> IREX higher education programs give individuals in the United States and overseas the resources and opportunities they need to conduct innovative social science and humanities research; increase their professional knowledge and abilities; and advance their leadership skills.

(http://www.irex.org/highered/research.asp,
accessed 23 January 2004)

Additionally, there are some supranational governmental organisations, such as the European Union, which have their own research funding arms and which fund strategic research. For example, the European Science Foundation funds strategic research and supports the pursuit of knowledge that does not necessarily have an action component:

> The European Science Foundation promotes high quality science at a European level. It acts as a catalyst for the development of science by bringing together leading scientists and funding agencies to debate, plan and implement pan-European initiatives.

> (http://www.esf.org/, accessed 23 January 2004)

It runs a scheme for the social sciences called the European Collaborative Research Projects in the Social Sciences (2001–2003) that, at the moment, involves co-operation between national research councils and the European Science Council. It describes its foci thus:

> The new scheme is open to applications on any topic within the social sciences that demonstrates an international framework for research collaboration. Projects need not be exclusively European in their topic focus. The scheme offers the opportunity to fund multilateral projects addressing international topics and issues pooling European research expertise. Project applications must involve collaboration amongst research teams in a minimum of three European countries. The scheme is designed to enhance the continuing process of European academic networking and career development by providing financing for problem-driven research projects to consolidate these achievements and trends. It offers the opportunity for researcher-led innovation in topic choice and directions for international research.

> (http://www.esf.org/, accessed 23 January 2004)

Government contract research

We mentioned above that there are two principal sources of government funding. We've dealt with that available through research councils and the like. The second main type of government funding is contract research. Because here the government is specifically 'buying' a piece of work, the research agenda is set and tightly prescribed by the funder. The subject of the research will generally be defined by reference to some 'policy need'. In the UK in particular, there is an increasing demand from government for what it calls 'evidence-based policy'. This is where government is supposedly setting policy agendas on the basis of 'evidence' rather than, say, ideology. This sounds good but, inevitably, because the research agenda is set by the funding organisation, such work often produces 'policy-based evidence'. In other words, the researchers almost inevitably end up telling the policy makers what they want to hear. Such work needs to be approached with some caution. However, it can provide a fruitful means of funding research and giving access where it might otherwise prove difficult.

Here are some of the ways in which you might get access to such funding.

- Some of these contracts are open to tender, advertised widely in newspapers and on government websites and are allocated according to competitive selection processes (although usually you do not get feedback on your application and the processes are not as transparent as one might like). Anyone or any team can apply, although clearly to win you have to be a credible applicant in terms of expertise and experience. It also might be the case, however, that the tender implies that certain sorts of research individuals or teams are preferred. Some government departments with major research programmes may operate an email alert service of upcoming tender possibilities.
- Some other government grants are put out to tender to selected individuals, organisations or institutions and the competition is more restricted. You should always try and get yourself on appropriate tender lists. Check with the organisation how to do this.
- Yet other grants are allocated to selected individuals or institutions.

The latter two cases tend to arise when trust relations have been built up between people in government circles and researchers, or when researchers have a strong reputation in the field and/or when they are understood to be in sympathy with the government agendas. These contracts can be more politicised than other government grants.

Government research funding of this sort is for contract research. There are several points to be alert to here. The contractor:

- Has greater power.
- Sets the specifications.
- Controls the expenditure.
- Establishes milestones and their associated 'deliverables'.

- Specifies outcomes.
- Controls the outputs (and may even decide not to publish your report).
- Monitors the contract – closely.

It follows that, if you undertake this sort of research, you must scrutinise the contract carefully and negotiate, where possible, before you sign anything – your university's legal adviser will assist you. You need to ensure that:

- You are very clear about what is expected at each stage.
- The research can be completed in the time-lines specified.
- You have clarified matters of intellectual property. This is a particularly contentious issue, which we address further below, but note that the contract may mean that you can neither speak publicly about the project until it is complete nor publish from it at all or until a certain time after completion. It may also mean that your name does not even appear on the report, or that the report gets buried.

We prefer to do this sort of research in teams. This is partly because the deadlines are usually so tight and you thus need lots of people on deck – particularly those who are prepared to work above and beyond the call of duty. Often such research contracts also call for multiple research skills, some of which you as an individual may not possess, and thus again teams are valuable. It is also useful to have various people to help you to liaise with those in government, as such liaison work can be very demanding, particularly if you're contracted to undertake research on a contentious topic.

Again, you must deliver what you say you will but you (and your team) are not usually alone in this responsibility. Often the government funder will have a management team that oversees the research and that considers each deliverable as it is submitted.

At the global level, a number of quasi-governmental inter- and supranational organisations (such as the OECD) provide funding for contract research. Their objectives in funding such research are usually associated with global or regional governance. As such, the funding is aligned to their primary 'mission'. For these bodies, strategic research is not the norm. Grants are usually available for specific development or action projects that mainly seek to directly address a particular issue and to effect change.

These grants usually require various complex partnership arrangements and are often restricted to specific countries. The various requirements for partnerships involve different public/private/civil society combinations, which tend to include:

- Local authorities.
- Local stakeholders.
- Non-governmental organisations (NGOs).
- Community organisations.
- Professional associations.
- International development organisations.

The World Bank is an example of a supranational organisation that funds research. Its website states:

> A limited number of grants are available through the Bank, either funded directly or managed through partnerships. Most are designed to encourage innovation, collaboration with other organizations, and participation by stakeholders at national and local levels.
>
> (http://web.worldbank.org/WBSITE/EXTERNAL/
> OPPORTUNITIES, accessed 23 January 2004)

Its list of grant categories includes those below.

Grant Resources for Civil Society Organizations

Describes a wide range of Bank-supported grant resources that are available to qualified organizations, including eligibility requirements and instructions for making applications.

InfoDev (http://www.infodev.org/projects/apply.htm)

A global program managed by the Bank to promote innovative applications of information and communication technologies, with ▶

▶ emphasis on meeting the needs of low-income communities in developing countries. The program pools intellectual, technical, and financial resources of public and private institutions from across the globe to assist promising projects and initiatives.

Social Funds

The Fund helps empower the poor and vulnerable by allowing them to become actively involved in the development of their communities. Typically, social funds develop into long-term poverty reduction and social capital creation mechanisms, with the objective of improving infrastructure, providing employment, community development, improving the delivery of social services and/ or supporting decentralization.

(http://web.worldbank.org/WBSITE/EXTERNAL/OPPORTUNITIES/ 0%2C%2CcontentMDK:20061756~menuPK:96315~pagePK:95 645~piPK:95672~theSitePK:95480%2C00.html+grants)

As you will see, in each such category a rather limited range of grants, scholarships, fellowships and study grants exists. Foci include capacity building, the environment, health, nutrition and population, education, information technology, poverty reduction and social development. We shall have more to say on the World Bank later.

International and transnational funding agencies sometimes name academic institutions and research institutes as possible recipients of research funds, but this is not usual and sometimes they may be actively excluded. Researchers from universities tend to become involved as a result of their networks or as consultants. They may undertake such things as case studies, surveys, policy analysis, pilot studies, feasibility studies, evaluations, research and non-research-based consultancies and may also be involved with organising and offering training activities.

Foundations and charitable trusts

What is a foundation or a trust? Basically, these are organisations established in order to administer funds of money. They are created in order to pursue certain stated objectives and are generally governed by a group of trustees or a board whose task is to ensure that the foundation or trust's income is managed well and applied as designated by the original benefactors. The benefactors can be (rich) individuals or corporations. The organisations usually hold substantial capital wealth and use the income from this capital in pursuit of the trust or foundation's purposes. This means that during times when stock market or interest rate returns are low, the income available for grants, etc., may also be commensurately reduced. A number of these organisations support academic research. Many foundations now have an increasing emphasis on public policy and social welfare and on action-oriented research.

The exact form of these organisations will vary according to the legal forms available in different countries, but you will know one when you see one. The Foundation Center's website (http://fdncenter.org/research) explains that there are two main types in American law, public and private, and elaborates on the differences between and within each category. Here are some extracts, which exclude small details not pertinent beyond the USA.

A private foundation

- is a nongovernmental, nonprofit organization;
- has a principal fund or endowment;
- is managed by its own trustees and directors;
- maintains or aids charitable, educational, religious, or other activities serving the public good;
- makes grants, primarily to other nonprofit organizations.

There are three different types of *private* foundations:

- *Independent* or *Family Foundations* receive endowments from individuals or families.
- *Company-sponsored* or *Corporate Foundations* receive funds from their parent companies, although they are legally separate entities.
- *Operating Foundations* run their own programs and services and typically do not provide much grant support to outside organizations.

▶

▶ *A public foundation*

- is a nongovernmental, nonprofit organization;
- receives funding from numerous sources;
- is managed by its own trustees and directors;
- operates grants programs benefiting unrelated organizations or individuals as one of its primary purposes;
- makes grants, primarily to other nonprofit organizations.

There are numerous types of *public* foundations:

- *Community Foundations* seek support for themselves from the public, but like private foundations provide grants. Their grants primarily support the needs of the geographic community or region in which they are located.
- *Women's Funds* – examples include the Los Angeles Women's Foundation, the Ms Foundation for Women.
- *Other Public Foundations* include funds serving other population groups and field-specific funds, such as health funding foundations.

(http://fdncenter.org/learn/classroom/ft_tutorial/ftt_part1_ q1.html, accessed 23 January 2004)

The Foundation Center website contains extensive information on private and public philanthropic foundations in the USA. Searches can be made for basic information of more than 70,000 private and community foundations. Searches, by subject or geographic key word, can also be made of annotated links to private foundations. It includes information on trends in grant expenditure and a list of the 100 largest US grant-making foundations ranked by spending.

Similar initiatives exist outside the USA. For instance, Funders Online is an initiative of the European Foundation Centre Orpheus Programme that operates from the European Foundation Centre (EFC). Orpheus, the information and communications programme of the EFC, provides a public information service on foundations and corporate funders active in Europe (http://www.fundersonline.org/). The Japan Foundation Center (http://www.jfc.or.jp/eibun/e_index.html) includes information on grant-making foundations in Asia and Oceania.

Some trusts are happy to respond to research proposals, whilst others are more proactive and have defined research agendas. These establish the parameters within which they would like to receive proposals. Foundations have a tendency to focus on particular fields. For example, in the USA the major foundations interested in education include the Ford, Rockefeller, Spencer, Macarthur, Pew, Markle, Gates, Atlantic, Pew and DavisVining Foundations.

All major trusts and foundations tend to have very good websites (after all, they are trying to give their money away) and may also have email alert services by means of which you can receive prompt notification of any special projects they wish to support or advance notice of major new programmes.

There are many funding agencies that are international foundations. Lists and details about these are readily accessed through the TGCI Grantsmanship Centre website (http://www.tgci.com/intl/index.asp) with its live links to International Funding Sources. The Asia Foundation is one such body and below is the programme page of its website.

The Asia Foundation

For 47 years, The Asia Foundation has sponsored and administered programs throughout Asia and in the U.S.

Programs by Subject – Information on Asia Foundation programs by subject matter, organized according to the Foundation's four primary areas of focus: Governance, Law, and Civil Society, Economic Reform and Development, International Relations, and Women's Political Participation.

The Foundation also has significant crosscutting programs in Information & Communications Technology (ICT) and the Environment.

Programs by Location – Information on Asia Foundation programs in:

Afghanistan – Bangladesh – Cambodia – China – East Timor – India – Indonesia – Japan – Korea – Mongolia – Nepal – Pakistan – Philippines – Sri Lanka – Taiwan – Thailand – Vietnam

▶ **U.S.-Administered Programs** – Information on U.S.-based programs, including the Asian-American Exchange Program, Books for Asia, Information & Communications Technology (ICT), the Luce Scholars program, Environment, and programs in Washington, D.C.

Project Lists – View all individual Asia Foundation projects by location and subject matter.
Grant Guidelines – View general information about Asia Foundation grant-making procedures.

(http://www.asiafoundation.org/ accessed 23 January 2004)

The private sector

University–industry research partnerships are not new, but with many nations attempting to develop so-called 'knowledge-based' economies this form of research funding is becoming increasingly significant. Indeed, it is being heavily promoted by governments and by universities. The former see it as way of achieving economic growth through the commercialisation of research and for the latter it is also a means of gaining access to non-government money. This trend now extends beyond the conventional science, technology, engineering and medical science industry–university partnership and also includes such partnerships in the social sciences and humanities.

In the past, the mechanisms for establishing links were largely informal and, unlike most of the funding sources we have already discussed, they were not generally accessed via a formal application process. Today, opportunities to forge links are increasingly supported by government programmes set up to foster and, sometimes, to co-fund collaboration. For instance, the Scottish Research Information System (www.scottishresearch.com/) promotes itself as the 'one-stop source linking industry and academic research in Scotland'. The Industry Canada website includes links to Industry Liaison Office in Canadian universities, technical institutions, teaching hospitals and colleges (http://strategis.ic.gc.ca/SSG/tf00135e.html). In Australia, the Australian Research Council co-funds university–industry partnerships through its Linkage grants scheme. The Australian commonwealth government funds the Cooperative Research Centre Program and is promoting access to this programme for small and medium businesses, although the centres are concentrated in the science and technology disciplines. Universities themselves are beginning to institute mechanisms for facilitating partnerships, offering advice and support to both university staff and industry partners. Below is an example from the University of Toronto.

UTech Services

The Innovations Foundation and University of Toronto's Technology Transfer office have joined forces to create UTech Services, an integrated storefront of services for industrial partnerships, technology transfer and commercialization. The staff of UTech Services includes:

- Specialists in contracts, agreements and negotiations
- A team of business development officers
- The staff of the Innovations Foundation, who are experts in licensing technology and fostering new spin-off companies

UTech Services helps researchers to:

- Identify potential industry partners
- Negotiate funding and intellectual property agreements
- Access government matching programs
- Seek legal protection for their intellectual property
- Comply with the university's policies
- Market and license inventions
- Access sources of seed and venture capital
- Create spin-off companies

(http://www.rir.utoronto.ca/utech/, accessed 23 January 2004)

The current promotion of research and development (R&D) in many countries creates a climate in which private corporations are open to opportunities for collaboration. However, they will fund only projects that are seen to meet their needs. It is worth while keeping in mind that, included among the key incentives to collaborate for industry, are strategic access to specialised research and development and the resolution of problems. Different forms of co-operative relationships include:

- The provision of technical and scientific training.
- Research.
- Consultancy.
- Services.

Industry may offer research funding as a cash grant as well as in-kind contributions such as:

- Material and expertise.
- Access to facilities.
- Services.
- Research 'subjects' – or, to put it more politely, participants or respondents.

Although university–industry partnerships are becoming more formal and structured, informal strategies for establishing a partnership remain important. These include personal networks. Academics with experience in industry may access opportunities via contact with former employers and co-workers or through contact with former contemporaries now working in industry. Participation in industry-focused conferences and participation on boards and consultative committees provide other means to develop informal networks.

Thinking globally again, many transnational organisations will also fund research. Keep in mind that these organisations are profit-motivated and that their provision of research funds is aligned to this. As part of the organisations' corporate social responsibility efforts they may establish a pseudo-foundation – an organisation that looks independent from the corporation but isn't necessarily so.

IBM is an example of a transnational organisation whose primary purpose is profit but which also awards funds as part of its 'corporate philanthropy'. For IBM 'Good Philanthropy is Good Business ...'. The fact that IBM's corporate giving helps the spread of its product demonstrates the point.

IBM corporate philanthropy spans the globe with diverse and sustained giving programs that support initiatives in education, workforce development, arts and culture, and the environment to benefit communities in need. IBM demonstrates its commitment to good corporate citizenship by providing grant recipients with technology, employee time and talent, and project funds.

(http://www.ibm.com/ibm/ibmgives,
accessed 23 January 2004)

Such philosophies translate into programmes of grants, as the following shows:

Grants program

To make the most effective use of IBM resources and expertise, IBM has selected priority issues and key initiatives for investment. Our main focus is Education. We also provide smaller grants in the areas of Adult Education and Workforce Environment. In addition, we provide opportunities for IBM employees to support their communities and the issues they care about through Employee Giving.

Education

IBM realizes the power and importance of education. Through major initiatives such as Reinventing Education, the IBM KidSmart Early Learning Program, and IBM MentorPlace, IBM is working to raise student achievement and enhance academic productivity to support thriving communities around the globe.

Adult training and workforce development

Technology can be a powerful tool in education and job training programs for adults, helping broaden opportunities and strength-ening programs available to adults in need of new skills and employment. It also can help simulate real job conditions, make the acquisition of education and skills more effective and help people get the network of support they need to obtain and retain employment.

▶ *Arts and culture*

IBM's support of the arts stems from our strong tradition of bettering our communities. We feel a deep sense of responsibility both inside and outside the company – a focused determination to enhance the communities in which we do business and in which our customers and employees live. By joining with libraries, museums, and other cultural institutions in exciting partnerships that leverage IBM expertise, we also demonstrate the critical role technology plays in enhancing the arts.

Helping communities in need

Wherever IBM does business around the globe, we form connections to communities and support a range of civic and non-profit activities that help those in need. In all our efforts, we demonstrate how technology can enrich and expand access to services and assistance.

Environment

IBM's support of the environment promotes the optimal use of leading-edge technology to conduct environmental research to offer new knowledge and enhanced understanding of these important issues.

Employee giving

IBM teams with employees to support organizations and causes in the communities where they live and work. Community-level grant making and extensive volunteer programs help our employees become personally involved in community projects.

(http://www.ibm.com/ibm/ibmgives/grant/, accessed 16 February 2004)

Checking out the ethics and politics

It's worth pointing out that all funding bodies have their own particular ethos. Sometimes this is clear from their websites but not necessarily, so you may need to check more widely. Take the case of the World Bank. It has a Social Fund which, as we have shown, provides funds for projects to support the poor and the vulnerable. But you may like to consider its commitment to such a social project given its other activities. Indeed, for critical and satirical comments on the World Bank go to The Whirled Bank at http://www.whirledbank.org/.

You would be well advised to try to check out the politics of the funding body you are considering, because you may:

- Be ideologically opposed to its politics and not wish to be associated with it – no matter what size the grant.
- Agree with its politics and thus be able to write the grant application in good faith.
- Attempt to be apolitical and simply wish to tailor your grant application accordingly so that it will be favourably assessed.

You should be aware that such politics, particularly but not exclusively in regard to corporate sponsorship, might generate ethical issues and dangers. These may be around findings with which the funder disagrees or around notions of 'commercial confidentiality', which prevent you publishing. If you are interested in the ethical basis of funding you need to check out not only what the funding body does (for example, do you want money from tobacco or arms producers?) but also what it supports (for example, political parties).

Getting the low-down on funders

You now have an idea about the nature of research funding, why you may actively seek funding and the main types of funding body. We now turn our attention to the pragmatic, if somewhat prosaic, subject of how to divine the kind of detailed information on funders that you will need to prepare yourself for making an application.

As well as knowing about the various sources and types of funding, you need to know how to readily access such information in a timely and time-saving manner. There are various ways to do this, and you might try any or all of the following:

- University/faculty research offices.
- The higher education press.
- The tender sections of newspapers.
- Professional knowledge (e.g. when you read papers in journals, or research reports in the press, check who the funding body is, as it is usually acknowledged).
- Personal contacts and informal sources: information can be gleaned through casual conversation, seminars, colleague review and contacting researchers in similar fields.

How can I find out about them?

The Web is a particularly useful source of information and you can use it in various ways. There are many websites, particularly US-based, which provide information on almost-everything-you-need-to-know about winning and managing research funding. A good example is the Foundation Center website (http://fdncenter.org/research), which, unlike many of its compatriots, does not charge for its on-line tutorials. You should obviously make yourself familiar with such sites, noting, however, that they are not necessarily aimed at early career researchers in the academy.

You should regularly visit the sites that you know. Take the example of government websites. The Australian commonwealth government publishes *GrantsLINK* (http://www.grantslink.gov.au), which provides information about commonwealth government grants and funding opportunities. The GrantsFINDER allows you to search for commonwealth government funding by subject, agency or grant name. Grants-LINK also includes links to state government entry points and commercial/non-government grant providers.

Looking for a grant from the Commonwealth Government?

GrantsLINK WILL HELP YOU FIND IT.

- **Getting Started**
Learn how GrantsLINK works, the types of grants the Commonwealth provides and get some general tips on completing your application form.

▶

▶

- **Search by keywords**
  Use the Quick Search to the left of your screen to find a grant by keyword. An **Advanced Search** facility is also available.

- **GrantsFINDER**
  Not sure what you should search for? Browse through a list of grants programmes organised by **subject agency** or **grant name**.

- **GrantsASSIST**
  Didn't find what you were looking for? A range of assistance is available through GrantsASSIST. You can contact **Commonwealth Regional Information Service** by calling us on (freecall) 1800 026 222 9am-6pm Mon-Fri AEST)

  (http://www.grantslink.gov.au/, accessed 23 January 2004)

You can also, of course, use various search engines to locate funding sources. After such a search you can focus on those possibilities that pertain to you and follow them up. For instance, if you type in 'international research grants' or 'international research opportunities', Google generates a helpful list. However, doing it that way is time-consuming and not necessarily timely in relation to funding timetables and deadlines. Fortunately, there are various other ways you can get information about funding opportunities, and the mechanisms available are becoming more and more sophisticated – particularly Web-based services. Consider IRIS, the Illinois Researcher Information Service.

IRIS is a unit of the University of Illinois Library at Urbana–Champaign. IRIS offers three Web-based funding and research services: the IRIS Database of federal and private funding opportunities in all disciplines; the IRIS Alert Service; and the IRIS Expertise Service. The IRIS Database currently contains over 8,000 active federal and private funding opportunities in the sciences, social sciences, arts, and humanities. Users can search IRIS by sponsor, deadline date, keyword, and other criteria. Most IRIS records contain live links to sponsor Web sites, electronic

▶

▶ forms, or Electronic Research Administration (ERA) portals. The IRIS Database is updated daily. Researchers at subscribing institutions can create their own IRIS search profiles and detailed electronic CVs ("biosketches") and post them to a Web-accessible database for viewing by colleagues at other institutions, program officers at federal and private funding agencies, and private companies.

(http://gateway.library.uiuc.edu/iris/, accessed 23 January 2004)

While this site is mainly for the USA, it does include hot links to government sites in other countries. It is also worth noting that whilst this site has open access for staff at the University of Illinois, its information is available to other colleges and universities only for an annual subscription fee. Similarly, the Foundation Center in the USA, which provides information on private foundations and corporate grants, charges users for its advice, as does Global Grant (http://www.globalgrant.com/). Grants Online (http://www.grantsonline.org.uk) also charges a subscription fee for its service, which includes a database of funding opportunities in the European Union and UK government and grant-making trusts.

Similar services exist at other selected universities in other countries. The University of Southern Queensland, for instance, provides access to the Grant Search Database (http://www.ourcommunity.com.au/funding/grant_search.jsp), which allows you to search Australian federal and state government, philanthropic and corporate grant funding options that are available in Australia. The Sponsored Program Information Network (SPIN), to which a number of Australian universities subscribe, also includes international funding sources.

InfOffice – SPIN, SMARTS & GENIUS

In the current economic climate, researchers have no alternative other than to look for industry and non-government sources for research dollars to support their work. Universities now have the benefit of three inter-related database services –   ▶

> ▶ **SPIN** (Sponsored Program Information network),
>
> **SMARTS** (Spin Matching and Research Transmittal System) and
>
> **GENIUS** (Global Expertise Network for Industry, Universities and Scholars).
>
> Each database not only assists with searching for alternative funding sources but will also help to foster networking.
>
> **SPIN** is an extensive database of potential funding sources both within Australia and overseas updated on a daily basis.
>
> **SMARTS** is an electronic matching and funding opportunity notification engine which provides investigators with direct and targeted information about relevant funding opportunities.
>
> **GENIUS** is a global database containing the expertise of researchers and scholars from universities and research organisations throughout the world. Profiles detailing expertise are created and maintained by researchers and scholars themselves. An increasing number of funding bodies and organisations are targeting individual researchers via the **GENIUS** database.
>
> (http://www.unisa.edu.au/orc/grants/infofficeinst.htm, accessed 23 January 2004)

If your university does not subscribe to such services, you might consider lobbying to get access to them – after all, it is in the university's interests that you are successful as a funded researcher.

Another way of getting information is through electronic or paper-based funding alerts. These:

- Are usually provided regularly.
- Can come to you as a newsletter.
- Include a range of funding opportunities such as funding for services and programmes as well as research.
- Have lists of available grants, agencies and deadlines and sometimes also indicate what/who has been funded in the past by particular funding bodies.
- Give details of:

- The grant provider.
- The grant scheme (including all the restrictions on topic and who is excluded).
- Funding amounts and limits. Usually a funding range is indicated.
- The closing date.
- Further information on the grant itself.
- Contact phone, fax numbers and email and Web addresses. They will usually hot-link you to the website of the provider so you can get information directly about the organisation and readily access and download the funding guidelines and application forms in Acrobat or PDF.

Easy Grants, Information Service in Australia puts out a newsletter monthly and it usually includes:

Part 1 – Summary and index of information
Part 2 – Updates, Hot Tips and the Search for Grant Information and Resources
Part 3 – This edition's Great Grant
Part 4 – Easy Grants in Detail

The grants covered by Easy Grants are grouped as follows:

Arts and Culture
Community Services
Sport and Recreation
Infrastructure
Philanthropic
Research
Environment and Heritage
Economic Development and Tourism
Technology and Telecommunications

Now that researchers have a much more global sensibility, it is very useful to use researcher information services that alert you to funds made available by providers beyond your national borders. The TGCI Grantsmanship Centre (http://www.tgci.com) provides hot-links to Funding Sources grouped as follows:

- Africa.
- Asia, Australia, New Zealand and the Pacific Islands.
- Canada.
- Central America, the Caribbean and South America.
- Europe.
- The Middle East.

Additionally, the TGCI centre offers 'grantsmanship' training and low-cost publications to non-profit organisations and government agencies. Its publications include *Winning Grant Proposals Online,* which collects the best of funded federal grant proposals annually and makes them available on CD-ROM, and a guide called *Program Planning and Proposal Writing.*

It will take you some time to check out all these information sources but, again, it is time well spent. The aim here is to become so familiar with them that using them becomes a habitual part of your research practice.

4 Getting the Basics in Place

In this chapter we help you to develop the basic skills you will require to put in winnable funding bids. We put this in the context of helping you to establish a grant-winning researcher identity.

Making choices

The way in which you have chosen to develop yourself as researcher and the institutional imperatives to which you are subject will frame the funding choices that you make. The options available will depend on your:

- Field of expertise.
- Research interests and those you wish to develop.
- Preferred research modality.
- Time and energy.
- Motivations and ambitions.
- Politics.
- National location.
- Institutional location.
- Networks.
- The possible research teams you may form or join.

In short, they will depend on your researcher identity.

Shaping up your image: funding and your researcher identity

Funding is so important to your development as a researcher that your choices about it should be an integral part of your decisions about the direction that you want your research career to take. Seeking and winning funds should be part of a continuing personal research development strategy for you and your research collaborators. It should not be an *ad hoc* or unprincipled grab for money. In planning your research directions carefully, sequentially and realistically you need to:

- Be highly focused.
- Be very strategic.
- Consider the ways in which all your academic activities interrelate and can benefit each other – in other words, the multiple pay-off effect.
- Consider how your research connects with other pertinent research in your university and the broader research and other communities with which you identify.

There are a number of questions (many of which are discussed in *Getting Started on Research*) to address:

- Who am I as a researcher?
- What is my main research focus and agenda?
- What are my medium and longer-term goals?
- In terms of those goals, what are my research strengths and what areas do I need to strengthen?
- What relevant networks do I have and which do I need to build? (See *Building Networks*.)
- What do I want to achieve in terms of identity, profile and research performance?
- What range of activities will get me there – what publications, research-related activities and links, for instance?
- How can I link my teaching and research?
- What might I have to give up to achieve this? Consider what you can legitimately say 'no' to at your workplace, when and how.

You can use your answers to these questions to construct a plan for yourself of the type shown as Table 1. We've made this one for three years – which is a sensible medium-term time frame. Such a plan should help you to systematically integrate your various academic activities with a view to steadily achieving your research objectives. We have filled in an imaginary example. It is best if you revisit your plan at least once a year and you may, indeed, be asked to do something like this by your department, faculty or university.

TABLE 1 Planning your research for the next three years

Year	Research grants (internal/external)	Publications	Collaboration with industry and/or international scholars	Research community activities (internal/external)	Connecting teaching and research	What can I say no to?
1	Apply for internal seed funding for a pilot project on gender and consumption. Examine EU websites and conditions for grant applications	From literature review for pilot, submit a review essay to *Journal of Gender Studies*	Make contact with proposed European partners and discuss possible collaboration with them. Link with key feminist scholars in field to explore ideas	Present conference paper laying out the issues for the proposed project	Speak to convenor of undergraduate and postgraduate taught degrees about possibility of teaching about gender and consumption. Develop courses and get them validated	Constant student demands on my time – allow only set times for students and make them keep to these except in the direst emergency. Don't let email eat up all my time
2	Carry out pilot study and write full application for European funding with academic partners in Europe. Apply internally and externally for funds to host visiting scholars	Revise article above and, from pilot study, write refereed journal article for *European Journal of Cultural Studies*	Work closely with selected EU partners on pilot study and to fully develop project proposal	Organise a seminar/colloquium with European partners	Begin teaching courses on gender and consumption. Speak to convenor of postgraduate research degrees about advertising for research students interested in gender and consumption	Continue as above and reduce the number of committees I serve on
3	With European partner universities, apply for EU research funds for big cross-national project on gender and consumption	Develop publishing plan linked with European proposal	Write up results from cross-national pilot study. Finalise proposal and put it in. Hopefully, begin research project with EU partners	Host European collaborators to visit my university as visiting scholars, including seminar series and 'master classes'	Continue under-graduate and post-graduate teaching and begin supervising in the area	Focus on project and refuse to review books or write chapters in edited collections unless they are related to my project

Try not to do this planning in isolation from your institution, especially if you are in the early stages of your career. You will need to work with and within the university on research funding bids, so talk to the relevant people and find out what the approval policies and procedures are and what financial and other support is available for formulating bids. Use any incentive schemes designed to encourage people to put in bids and see what administrative support is available to assist with budgets, formatting and the like, or research assistance to help with chasing references, typing up bibliographies and so on.

Hopefully, such planning exercises will let you identify your research funding needs and help develop a strategy for getting what you want. Your plan needs to be flexible enough to allow you to include new knowledge and relevant opportunities but also sufficiently firm to prevent you whimsically taking off in all directions and responding to opportunities that are tangential.

Who will find me attractive?

Having done your strategic planning, you will need to give serious consideration to precisely locating the funding bodies that have the greatest congruence with your research plans over the short to medium term. Consider a possible range of potential funders across:

- Those agencies that fund researcher-initiated projects and those that fund projects they have initiated themselves.
- Public and private funders.
- National, international, transnational and supranational bodies.

Be neither too humble nor too ambitious and be realistically optimistic. Having a good mix of target funders will enhance your chances of winning at least something, and your diverse successes will also look good on your CV. Remember that one type of grant can feed into another type, providing you with 'multiple pay-offs'.

In developing your plan, it may make sense to start with Mode II funding from your university, if at all possible. The competition will be less severe and you will be able to develop the kind of 'grantsmanship' skills that you will need with external funding bodies. Moreover, such funding will enable you to build up your research management experience, conference presentations and publications – all of which will make you look more credible as someone who 'delivers' in the eyes of external funders. This is called the elevator effect.

When you turn your attention to external funders you should compile a list of key agencies with which you would like to develop a relationship. You might do this alone or with your research collaborators. If you have access to research assistance, such people may do the work for you. Alternatively, a good research administrator in your school, department, faculty or university may well be able to help – but you will need to brief them carefully. Even if you do have help with this work, it is ultimately down to you to refine your list, as the idea is to tailor it to your plans.

Your university's research website should be a good starting point, as others may have made a start with collecting the kind of information that you want. Rather than just 'bookmark' websites, document your list of potential funders in a chart similar to Table 2 . This illustrates the sorts of things that you need to be very clear about, and documenting them like this aids clarity. It may seem like an awful lot of work, but you only need to do it once from scratch. However, you do need to update it regularly, because funders change. For instance, the fact that the value of stocks and shares fell dramatically during the 1990s and early twenty-first century means that foundations (and often universities too) have less money to distribute and they may thus have tightened their criteria. And of course, their main concerns and foci change over time as different issues emerge. As you get to know your funding agencies you will not bother with some, and others will require only minor alterations year on year.

Dating is important

Next, you need to construct a formal funding calendar. Because funders' dates are often immovable, you may have to integrate other, more flexible, activities around them. Important things to factor in are listed below.

- All dates fixed by the funder. Remember too that many funding bids may involve important dates after the initial submission – for

TABLE 2 Recording friendly funding agencies

	Details
Agency	
Contact details	
Key personnel	
Funding calendar	
Are submissions at any time or are there deadlines?	
Dates of the notification of outcomes and, if in stages, these dates	
Current concerns and foci	
Preferred knowledge (basic or applied research; disciplinary or interdisciplinary research)	
Preferred recipients, partnerships and restrictions	
Average allocations and expectations re co-funding	
Application process	
(expressions of interest or full applications)	
Politics (note the language used)	
Agency priorities	
Attitude to intellectual property	
Ethical issues	
Assessment criteria: summary only	

instance, you may be asked to submit a fuller proposal or respond to referees' evaluations.

- Time to integrate valuable feedback from your colleagues and mentors before the bid is submitted.
- Most universities and other institutions have a range of institutional processes for submitting grant applications, and you need to factor them into your own timetable. They may include getting the signature of senior colleagues, having the university legal adviser check any legal issues, having business managers check your budget, gaining preliminary ethics clearance and so forth. And, if you are working in a cross-university team or a cross-institutional team that involves outside partners, remember you will dealing with the

procedures of more than one institution. This considerably complicates the task.

- Also keep in mind that the bidding process, especially in the final stages, can be very time-consuming. You will have to do things such as putting things into the agency's format, producing multiple copies of your document, getting innumerable university signatures and complex on-line submission processes. You should never under-estimate how long this last stage will take. It is a well known and universal law that as deadlines hover ever closer, computers, photo-copiers, fax machines and email links all break down. And key personnel such as technicians or signing authorities are suddenly unavailable or difficult to reach. So on no account leave anything to the last minute. We promise you will rue the day if you do.

- Universities and research councils are the main funders of *researcher-initiated* research. This means you can begin planning submissions to such bodies far ahead of the due date. Fixed submission dates can be a good discipline – when the UK Economic and Social Research Council abolished fixed submission dates for smaller grants the number of applications dropped, possibly because academics no longer organised themselves to meet essential deadlines and 'just let things slip' instead.

You should always, where possible, try to create ample time for bidding activities, rearranging commitments well in advance if necessary. If you are bidding as part of a team, consider how you and your colleagues' diaries may be synchronised. For instance, you may be able to do the early leg work while your research colleague is on leave, and then pass the next stage of the process over to that person while you take leave. And finally, unlike Anita in the story below, always give people you want to help you plenty of advance notice and time.

Anita had completed a superb PhD and, over the subsequent year, had a number of articles accepted in peer-refereed journals. Towards the end of the year, she decided she wanted to apply for a research council grant based on an area of interest arising from her PhD. She also decided that she would like the support of some senior academic ▶

▶ colleagues in putting her bid together. The applications were due in early March but she didn't contact these colleagues until late January. Needless to say, none of them was available and she was unable to put in her application. She was advised by one of them to spend a year preparing her application properly and consulting people about it and to submit it the following year, perhaps after conducting a small project.

When you have completed your research plan, you will have a calendar for the year which at a glance will tell you what bids you are applying for and the time you have set aside to write the various applications.

What about unexpected chances?

Your calendar will not be able to include the funding possibilities that arise unexpectedly. These are often *contract* research opportunities. For instance, on your (regular) visits to, say, the government's website you may learn that it has suddenly decided to throw a lot of money at your area of interest. While you may have a general sense of what your government is likely to fund, you cannot always predict precisely what it will be and when. Because of the short time frame for such contracts, you will need to make a quick decision about whether to bid or not. Our advice is that unless this is the grant to die for (loads of money, time and potential impact), think hard before immediately dropping everything else in order to bid for it. You will need to consider the implications of such a contract for any other on-going work that you have. You may have to postpone other work you had planned or seek extensions of deadlines – all of which may be difficult to recover from if you keep responding to potentially dangerous but delicious opportunities. If you can't head up such a bid, you may have colleagues who can and who will involve you in some manageable way. If that is the case let them know of your availability but also of the limits of your time and take it from there. Above all, don't be like Bruce in the following story and let such work mess up your career.

Bruce is a mature-age academic who, for years, has been trying to complete a PhD in the history and philosophy of science. When he concentrates on his PhD he is inspired and motivated to complete. However, opportunities for funding keep arising and he can't resist them. Because he is particularly clever and in high demand, he also keeps winning them. This means that his PhD is constantly on hold. His publications mostly take the form of project reports, so he is not in a position to get a PhD by publication. Unfortunately for Bruce, his lack of a PhD and, in a sense, his lack of discipline and inability to prioritise his own interests and work meant that recently he missed out on promotion.

When is enough enough?

A number of people we know put their hands up for lots of bids in the hope that they will get as many as they can – or at least one. Depending on who they are and how much expertise they mobilise this has various consequences, which include the possibility of:

- Winning them all and thus facing the difficulty of completing them all. They run the risk of compromising the quality of the final product as well as their mental health.
- Winning none because they have concentrated on the quantity of their applications at the expense of the quality.
- Getting a reputation either as an outstanding success or the academic equivalent of a lawyer–ambulance-chaser.

The basic rule here is don't be greedy and only ever submit winnable bids. It's worse to put in rubbish than nothing at all in reputational terms. Moreover, bids take up serious amounts of time and effort, and if you are not selective and strategic you are wasting your efforts.

Learning from old hands

It is important to gain a sense of what a successful bid for a particular funder looks like. Where possible, look at successful and unsuccessful applications made by others and try to work out the reasons for the funder's decisions. Keep in mind, however, that some very good bids do not get funded simply because of the highly competitive nature of bidding to some research councils. Conversely, some rather ordinary bids do get funded for reasons other than what you may see as merit. Some websites include abstracts of successful applications, and it is useful to see what has won in the past and to try and work out the reasons why.

Getting fresh ideas

Okay, you have decided on your main research focus and agenda, targeted appropriate funding bodies and drawn up a funding calendar. The next major challenge is to generate winnable bids. Where do you go for additional ideas to help ensure that others see your proposed project as worthwhile? This will depend on your researcher identity and where you want your research to have impact. Clearly, we can't cover all bases here but we can give two examples from which you can generalise to your own research agendas. For further ideas we refer you to *Building Networks*.

First, if you work in a vocational or professionally oriented field of study such as education, health, sport, tourism or the law, you may seek recognition as a researcher who contributes in a very practical way to that field. If so, you will need to keep in touch and up to date with what is going on in that field, professionally as well as academically. You might do so in the following ways:

- Serve on professional bodies such as peer review panels, journal review boards or any other professional or academic body.
- Undertake some professional field experience.
- Read the academic and professional literature.
- Interact with others in various locations in the field.
- Read recent public reports and other public documents.
- Monitor social trends, legislation or agency goals.

If you are in a discipline without such a professional or practitioner orientation the sources that may help you (as well as professionally oriented academics) include:

- Casual conversations.
- Seminars.
- Colleagues' review of your work.
- Discussions with researchers in similar fields.
- Your reading.

All these are activities during which ideas for specific projects will constantly arise, and, given your close engagement with the field, they are highly likely to be seen as topical and relevant.

Making yourself irresistible

Producing a winnable bid involves two things, a quality project and quality applicants. So, what you and your research team look like on paper matters.

As the planning exercise we've outlined implies, looking good on paper does not happen overnight or serendipitously. It requires you to be very focused on getting a record, a profile and a reputation in your field. Some academics do so via a more traditional route and gain kudos through the publication of books, in peer-refereed journals and by focusing on winning research council grants. Others concentrate on professional or practitioner publications (for instance, reports and articles in professional journals) and seek much more *contract* research funding. Yet others do a lot of consulting work and 'leverage' their research grants off that. In most of these cases such people get out and about doing such profile work as conference presentations or running workshops and seminars. Of course, many people's research careers involve various combinations of these pathways.

Keep in mind that what looks good to one funding body may not look so good to another and that no-one expects people at the start of their research career to have a monumental CV. However, whatever your stage, you must be able to demonstrate that you are doing interesting and valuable research and disseminating the results.

Looking good as an individual is not the same as looking good as a team. Whilst funding bodies may have different preferences, usually the teams viewed most favourably have different but complementary research records and cover the range of knowledge and skills required for the project. A history of successfully completed projects, even if only among some of the team, also helps.

The most important thing, however, is to have a well designed project proposal which is tightly written, responsive to the particular needs or priorities of the hoped-for funder, and persuasive about the value of your research. *Getting Started on Research* goes into some detail on how to write research proposals.

Notching up a record

You should build a funding portfolio consisting of:

- Your up-to-date CV. See *Building an Academic Career* for advice on how to put this together.
- All your grant applications (even the unsuccessful ones).
- All your reports to funding bodies.
- All the feedback you have received on them – informal or formal, positive and negative.

There are many reasons for keeping all this stuff, either in electronic or in paper form (or even both).

- You can cut, paste or adapt from earlier applications – bibliographies, CVs or whatever.
- You can reuse earlier formatting.
- If you are reapplying to a funder you can readily remind yourself of the feedback you got last time.
- Invitations to tender for *contract* research are often at very, very short notice. If you have something 'on the stocks' which could be adapted quickly and easily, all the better (but don't feel you have to tender just because you've been invited to and have something there you can use – remember the story about Bruce, above).

Having all your application information together in one folder and structured by year and by organisation is a sensible way to organise this aspect of your research files. Part of being a successful researcher is having a filing system not just for each individual project but also for your overall research record. Apart from anything else it helps you to avoid the anxiety generated by chaos, but also being well organised saves you time in the long run. Have a chat to your research colleagues and see how they organise and archive their research.

In this chapter we have identified some of the important foundations of good research funding practice. In the next chapter we tell you everything you might ever want to know about the bidding process itself.

5

Getting Down, Dirty and Detailed

In this chapter we will help you to think about how you can set about the process of actually applying for money. We will talk about and give you our best advice on the various decisions and activities involved.

Where now and where next?

At this point you have:

- An emerging record, profile and reputation – you are looking good.
- An overall sense of your research directions.
- A specific plan for your research career over the next three years.
- A good knowledge of who funds what sort of research, of their priorities and specifications and of what a good bid looks like in the circles you want to move in.
- A funding calendar that matches your plan.

You have covered all the basics. Now let us get down to the very focused practice of winning a research grant. In the context of all the above you will have done one or more of the following things:

- Identified the funder whose money you want.
- Seen a project opportunity advertised that you wish to bid for.
- Been invited to tender for a project.
- Been invited to join a research team bid.
- Chosen wisely.

And where to next? The next main sets of decisions and activities include (1) deciding whether to work alone or in a team, (2) attending to the funder's specifications, (3) routine but important tasks, (4) higher-order conceptual work, (5) dealing with time, timetables and reporting requirements, (6) doing the budget. We will now deal with each in some considerable perhaps even pedantic detail. But as we said, this is about getting down, dirty and detailed.

Deciding whether to work alone or in a team

Choosing whether to go for a bid alone or in a team is a big decision and there are costs and benefits involved. Let us take some scenarios to enable us to explain these.

> Joe is an early career researcher. He has behind him a successful PhD in criminology, a few publications and the odd consultancy. He is a new member of a successful research centre and has been invited by the director to be part of a team bidding for a research council grant. The team includes some experienced grant winners and some early career researchers with a record similar to his. The topic involves empirical research and is not quite in his space but he can see where his ideas might fit into the overall project and how he might make a contribution.

Should Joe accept the invitation? Yes, is the simple answer. The team is strong and complementary, the questions the research is to address are fresh and exciting and the bid will have a strong chance of getting funded. If it is, Joe will get a foot on the first step of the funded researcher ladder. That will make it easier for him to get another grant later on. Further, being part of strong and experienced research team is a good induction into the process of winning and managing research grants. It also links him with his research colleagues in the research centre. While the actual research topic is not quite his, there is plenty of space for him to make a contribution, and he sees opportunities for taking this work more clearly in his own direction at a later date. In fact, even if the grant does not get funded, he will have had the benefit of learning how such a grant is prepared and of working closely with a group of colleagues.

Mary is an Indigenous researcher and one of few Indigenous academics with a PhD, which she has just completed while working as an academic. She is building up her research project experience by seeking internal university funding for collaborative action-oriented research projects and has chosen to undertake these projects with people she trusts in Indigenous communities. She has given quite a number of well-received conference papers out of these projects and is in the process of turning them into publications for refereed and other journals. In the following year she plans to bid for the research council money that is earmarked for Indigenous researchers. She is approached by a big multi-state high profile research team and is invited to join them to bid for a large government grant to study violence in Indigenous communities. The rest of the team is non-Indigenous but with a strong record of winning grants on gender and violence.

What should Mary do? This is a hard one. Or is it? The topic is important and certainly the money and the potential profile are enticing. However, Mary does not know the people, the lack of other Indigenous researchers on the team is a problem, and the project does not appear to have the action orientation that Mary is committed to. There is a danger that Mary will get swamped by the size and seniority of the research team and that she will be distracted from her own research agenda. The team has given her no indication that it is aware of the ethics of undertaking Indigenous research. It is thus probable that she will have to teach them about this aspect. Further, she and we have a sneaking suspicion that she has been included in the bid only because she will serve as the legitimisation device for a white research team. Our view is that Mary should not accept the invitation because not only does it interrupt her own research agenda, but more important, it is also in conflict with her research priorities and principles. It also appears that others wish to use her. She might instead build her own team on the basis of the principles she believes in and with the people she knows and trusts while at the same time making a strong case that research of this sort should be collaborative, action-oriented and involve Indigenous researchers and communities.

Prior to completing her PhD in record time Sarah had a career in the public sector and while there led a number of research projects on urban housing and poverty. She published quite extensively in research journals from her PhD and won some prizes and grants for international conference travel on the basis of these publications. These and also her links with industry resulted in her winning a postdoctoral position. Whilst doing her postdoc she undertook some consultancies for the housing industry and participated in research project teams within the research centre she was appointed to, all the while continuing to publish.

Should Sarah try to win a research council grant by herself? We say yes. This is in part because the research council in her country allocates some grants to early career researchers but also because Sarah's record means she is competitive in this field. She has a strong publication record, strong research team experience, including the experience of leading research projects. Her prizes and awards indicate that her more senior peers consider her outstanding. She has a winning record and all she now needs to do is produce a winnable bid.

Barry has just got a teaching post; his new PhD received rave reviews. His examiners have invited him to join international conference symposia, and, through them, others have invited him to write chapters for their books in his field and a reputable book publisher has offered him a contract. He is a widely and wisely read and charismatic academic and although new to his post is being courted by more senior academics at his university to join their research project teams. None of these offers has much to do with his research agenda but the projects are interesting and the prospect of working with at least one of the professors in his faculty is attractive because it provides him with mentoring opportunities. Also, and quietly, he does find it rather difficult to refuse someone so senior. However, his teaching load is huge and he is struggling to find time to publish from his PhD let alone to do new research.

What is our advice to Barry? We want to say first that most academics can recognise hot talent when they see it. Some seek to promote talented people by opening up opportunities for them to flourish in their own right. Others seek to harness that talent to their own agendas, and some do so in the guise of mentoring. Talented new researchers need to be wary of being co-opted in this way. They also should know that they need not take the first opportunities that arise just because they are there. We think Barry would be well advised to resist all offers to join research teams and to take all the opportunities available to him to publish out of his PhD. Further, when he does apply for a grant it should be on his own terms. Others are likely to want to join any team he develops because he has so much to offer but he should lead the ideas. However, given his high teaching load and his relative inexperience of managing a funded research project, he may want to form a team that includes others whom he knows and trusts and whose experience compensates for his inexperience.

We could go on with examples here but the overall point is that each case must be taken on its merits and there are few hard-and-fast rules. You must decide what is best for you, but remember, there are many traps for inexperienced players and you need to weigh up your choices in the light of your:

- Record.
- Research plans.
- Research agenda.

Do not get sucked into other people's agendas if they do not fit in with yours. We suggest you take advice from a trusted and *disinterested* mentor. The general rule is to choose your project partners very carefully.

With teams there are titles and hierarchies. Team members can be full or associate members – sometimes called chief investigators (CIs) and partner investigators (PIs). Confusingly though, the person leading the team may also be called a principal investigator (PI) and the others may be regarded as co-applicants. You need to be aware of what the acronyms in your particular situation mean. There is obviously a hierarchy here but there may also be hierarchies among the CIs. Often the funder wants a contact person named, and sometimes that person is called the Principal Investigator or First CI. Sometimes the grant goes through that person's university, and it gets the Brownie points and any associated infrastructure money – though sometimes it can be split between universities. This is quite a sensitive matter and must be carefully negotiated in the preliminary stages of pulling a team together.

Teams sound complicated. Why should I bother?

In general, the benefits of team research are that you can:

- Include people across disciplines, universities, other institutional sites including international locales. This can broaden the scope of the topic.
- Share the load.
- Get intellectual and other input from various people.
- Always have someone to talk problems through with.
- Learn heaps from others.
- Write and present at conferences in teams.

Further, as a junior researcher, you can get your feet wet without too much risk and can learn a host of things from senior members of the team.

There are, however, many difficulties and questions that can arise in relation to team membership. For example:

- Who is to be the chief and who are associate investigators?
- Which university should manage the grant? Often this is defined by where the first chief or principal investigator works. Think hard on this one.
- The uneven distribution of load, credit and visibility.
- The authorship of publications and ownership of ideas.
- Power struggles that arise around different agendas.
- Rivalry and envy within the team.
- Thoughtless or cliquey behaviour by team members.
- Teams are time-consuming, all decisions take much longer and even matching the diaries of very busy members can be a serious headache – ask any of our research assistants.

The benefits of individual research projects are that you avoid the above difficulties – although not totally, as some may arise in relation to the research associates or assistants you employ on the project. The difficulties associated with individual research projects include the lack of collegial input and support. However, research associates or assistants (RAs) can help to fill this gap. And there are other choices. Although you may choose to do the research alone you may develop a team with which you consult, for example. Or you may include PhD students or a postdoctoral position in your funding application. If you are considering developing projects with industry partners, it is worth remembering that the main reasons industry wants to be involved with research, apart from access to trained experts, is access to potential employees, so its important to include students who could be potential employees in the research proposal if you are chasing funding from industry.

Keep in mind, of course, that some funding bodies expect or give priority to team research and insist on various sorts of research partnerships. So, you may not have a choice about whether to team or not to team, unless you choose not to be funded by such bodies.

Having decided whether you want to work by yourself or with others, you need to get stuck into the all-important task of actually writing your funding application.

Attending to the funder's specifications

These specifications must be imprinted on your consciousness all the while you are doing the application. If you have done as we suggested above you will have a list of the funder's specifications. You will know their:

- Priorities – general and current specific.
- Inclusions re research approach (basic or applied) and discipline.
- Exclusions and restrictions over what and who they will not fund.
- Expectations re co-funding.
- Attitude to intellectual property.
- Ethical and political base.
- Average allocations.
- Application format and process.
- Assessment processes and criteria.
- Deadlines.

When writing applications make sure that, without exception, you clearly address the funder's specifications and follow their document format. Yes, right down to the suggested font and margin size if need be. They will throw your bid out if you do not. Indeed, it is usually the case that funding committees process so many applications they are looking for reasons to eliminate some to make the selection process less onerous. So don't make it easy for them to drop your bid off their pile.

We are surprised by the number of people we know who make plenty of applications for funding but never get in touch with people associated with the funding body. We think it is important to have a certain level of personal contact. It is still a good idea to make personal contact with the programme or grant officers. Try for a face-to-face visit or at least a phone call and have a list of topics ready just to clarify that your understandings are correct and that there have been no last-minute changes to their specifications. However, the main reason for the contact is to check out whether the direction you are taking is 'on target': whether there is anything more you can glean, need to know or can do.

Routine but important tasks

We suggest that at the outset of the application process you identify the routine tasks to be done. These include:

- *Assembling the team's track record.* This includes team members' CVs, their previous project reports, bibliographies, statements about project management histories. The track record is often assessed alongside the project itself. So don't be a slouch on these matters. As always, do not leave these things to the last minute. And, when you get requests for such information from your colleagues, answer them promptly.
- *Developing your publishing plan and dissemination strategy.* They may include the conferences, journals and publishers you plan to 'target', the development of a website, a media strategy and workshops or seminars for the profession. These should not be randomly thrown together or thought about just in an opportunistic manner but rather constructed carefully in relation to the purposes of the project and the audiences or 'end users' it seeks to reach.
- *Selecting codes and key words* if these are required in your application. The funders will often use such codes and key words to

choose reviewers of your application from their electronic database. Just as crucially, these words may determine which category of application your bid will be seen to belong to and thus who your competition is. This is a particularly difficult issue if you are doing interdisciplinary work. Some disciplines have cultures that are particularly punitive and super-critical. If you have the choice not to put down a code for a discipline you know to be like that, then make that choice.

- *Nominating a list of referees from which the funder might choose.* This list might only include academics or might also include 'users'. Choosing referees requires you to be strategic: so choose people who know your work or who will at least speak favourably about it in an informed and apparently disinterested manner. You also need to pick people who you know will honour this obligation. However, it is not a good idea to choose anyone who is too close to you, for they might be seen as having a conflict of interest. The referees must be seen to be both expert and detached. It is acceptable, indeed a courtesy, to contact your chosen referees before putting their names forward. You might send them an abstract of the bid and let them know the times they are likely to be called on. They can then let you know if they are willing and available. For many applications you will not have the opportunity to suggest a referee. However, it is useful to know that these may be chosen from your bibliography. So, it is not a good idea to include in your bibliography people who are likely to suggest politely that your work is unmitigated drivel that should be consigned to the compost heap without further ado. You should check your bibliography for such people, and consign them to the compost heap without further ado. The following story is an example of one way of being strategic with regard to your referees.

Davina, whose field is cultural studies, found that her research council bids were frequently being sent to mainstream psychologists for review. These reviewers were totally out of sympathy with the cultural studies paradigm and would usually trash her proposals on the grounds that the study was not 'scientific' or 'verifiable'. While ▶

▶ receiving one such review among a set of superlative ones did not necessarily prevent her from getting grants, Davina felt that it was a potential danger. She therefore made a habit of naming critical social psychologists whom she knew to be sympathetic to her theoretical frameworks whenever she was asked to nominate reviewers. This meant that the research council did not feel the need to obtain further reviews from psychologists.

- *Getting accompanying letters of support* from those to whom you need access and who are potential users of your research. Again lead time is crucial, as it is often the case that those who are to write these letters have to go through many layers of their own organisation to get them written and signed off. The letters can be just standard communiqués and sometimes that is all the funder permits. However, if the funder makes no such stipulation it cannot hurt if you make some suggestions about the text. Indeed, the authors of such letters may welcome a draft that they can they modify. Some of your carefully chosen words in their mouths can only be to your advantage.

- *Meeting the word length requirements and formatting the document.* Some Not Very Smart people try to fudge the length and seek to cram as much into the bid as possible by using a small font, reducing the size of the font or the spacing or widening the margins of their text. No. No. No. The formatting needs to look professional and the text must be easy to read. Indeed, the aesthetics of the document are important, so you should also avoid too many headings and sub-headings and sub-sub-headings and indents and dot points and numbered points and diagrams. Go for simple elegance in your headings rather than *italics* and **bold** and underlining and shading and different sized text or various **fonts** or Upper and Lower Case. Also try to balance the length of the various parts of the text. Some funding body headings require less text than others, so you need to work out which these are and get the balance right. Your diagrams should help to explain to the reader what you are seeking to do and should be easily understood. Of course the grammar and spilling must be impekable. A slapdash bid gets on assessors' nerves and negatively disposes them towards the applicant.

- *Getting feedback on your application* once you have a good draft available. (Don't waste people's time looking at very early drafts.) Often universities will organise sessions where you can take along your draft proposals and workshop them with other colleagues. Also, where possible get feedback from experienced and successful researchers or at the very least several critical friends. Give them enough time to enable them to do a jolly good read and for you to do jolly good revisions once you have the feedback. And, if you win the funds, let those who assisted you know. Offer some form of reciprocity. (We like money best but we are also happy with expensive meals or theatre tickets.) You should, for example, offer to read your colleagues' funding applications if you are asking them to look at yours.
- *Being your own best critic.* We do not mean here that you have to self-flagellate, talk yourself down and eventually cower in a corner in a foetal position. We mean that you must be able to get a certain distance from your work and to evaluate it critically in the same way you would any other person's. A bit of ruthless self-appraisal never goes astray as long as you follow it though with massive corrections and revisions and maybe ingest loads of chocolate at the same time.
- *Jumping through your university's hoops.* It has procedures that must be complied with before bids can be submitted to the funding body. Many universities like to check research grant applications, and this drives many researchers crazy because it is yet another deadline to meet. But if you want to produce winning bids it is important to have the support of finance departments, research officers and the like. They can often give you some handy hints to improve aspects of your grant. They also often find strange glitches in your budgets. So do not treat them only as bureaucratic functionaries there just to make life difficult – although some may be and may well do so.

The dean of research at a New Zealand university chose the following method to improve the quality of research grant applications in her university. She insisted that all colleagues prepared their grant applications well in advance and then subjected them to an appraisal process of precisely the same nature as that used by the research

▶ council. While her colleagues were rather irritated at being put under this pressure, they ultimately found the process very generative and success rates improved markedly.

- *Completing the final checklist* which is available to assist you to ensure you have jumped through all the required hoops. Having sat on numerous funding committees we know that many people do not use these lists and leave out much of the detail that is required by the funding body. Hard to believe but true. These checklists may save your bacon. *Use them.*

So who gets to do this work?

If you are developing a bid by yourself you will find that these routine tasks are not too onerous. But once you are in a team they get complicated and time-consuming. Some of the work might be given to a research assistant but not all of it. This is because it still often requires some academic judgement in relation to the priorities and specifications of the funding body. For instance, some funding bodies only ask people to include in their list of publications work that is peer-refereed. Bids that accidentally or otherwise include work that is not peer-refereed in such lists run the risk of being seen as either incompetent or as an attempt to fudge the record. Not nice either way. When there are tight word limits, which there usually are, further judgement is required and only the most relevant work should be included. Take another case. Your research grant track record needs to demonstrate that you are reliable, that you deliver the goods and on time. Your remarks on the team need to be more then mere reportage but should point out, convincingly, to the funder or assessor that it is a dream team with a unique and exciting blend of the talents and skills necessary to produce an outstanding result.

Higher-order conceptual work

The sort of higher-order conceptual work required to produce a winning bid will depend on the type of research grant. And so we need to say a bit about that, before we can return to the focus of this section.

Earlier we mentioned that research grants can be divided into different categories on the basis of different criteria. These include sponsored and contract research, which we defined in Chapter 2. What you need to know in this context is that funding for sponsored research is allocated competitively, usually on the basis of peer review. The intellectual property of the research usually remains with the researchers and their university. Contract research, on the other hand, may be awarded on the basis of competitive bidding but the selection process does not usually involve peer review. The outcomes of such projects tend to be seen in terms of the benefit to the funder, who usually owns the intellectual property but may be prepared to negotiate on how they exercise their rights.

These are loose categories and the specifications of funders can lead to variations. For instance, in the case of sponsored research there are situations where the funders provide categories within which researchers develop their own projects. In other words the researchers are not totally free to dream up their own research topics: to undertake what might be called 'curiosity-driven' research. Rather, their curiosity is framed by the funder. Often foundations sit in this ambiguous space. In such circumstances researchers may not be assessed by their peers and may be assessed by other experts. Equally, governments or industry may choose to fund basic research and to employ academics to peer-review such research.

As you can see there are lots of variables at work here and clearly what constitutes a winning bid will vary accordingly. Hence it is difficult to give generic advice. However, for the purposes of this exercise we will work with the categories employed above, keeping in mind that they are rather pure forms with lots of mutations.

If you are seeking to win a sponsored research grant your assessors will use a number of criteria to judge your bid.

- You will be expected to *show that you know your stuff*. Your bid should demonstrate that you are on top of your field and topic. It must be evident that you know the key debates, issues and authors pertinent to your chosen topic. However, when you demonstrate this, the assessors expect to see more than a condensed literature review or (shudder) a literature summary. They expect to see a distinctive, sophisticated and critical take on the issues.
- You need to *establish the warrant* or *rationale* for your project. Your peer assessors want to be persuaded by your warrant, they

want to know why they should give a damn. They will be persuaded not by mere assertion or indeed by hyperbole or rhetoric, but rather by systematically marshalled argument and evidence. There are many ways of justifying the worth of your project and you should look them up in *Getting Started on Research* if you feel you need guidance on how to do it. It is sometimes helpful if you can show the significance of your idea and you familiarity with the area through a previously conducted 'needs assessment' or pilot study on your topic.

- Your bid should also *demonstrate that you have a good research question that is worth asking* – that is, it is significant. In *Getting Started on Research* we talk about writing good research questions and so we will not repeat the points here. The questions should also be answerable and likely to be answered by the proposed project. You must be able to show clearly that the research approaches or methodologies that you adopt and the theories that you mobilise can do the job laid out in the aims and questions of the project. We are constantly astonished by the number of research proposals we see where the aims of the project do not match the questions and where the methods employed cannot address either. Your research application is a winner only if the project is do-able. And you must convince the assessors of that.

- You will be expected to *show that you know your methodological stuff* too. Again, the assessors expect you to demonstrate a critical awareness of the key methodological debates, issues and authors pertinent to your chosen theories and research techniques. And they expect your theories and your research techniques to be well integrated and compatible. For instance, although positivist methods do not sit well with post-positivist theories, you would be surprised how many people seem to think it is perfectly fine to unproblematically blend the two. Needless to say the bids from such applicants go down in a screaming heap.

- You need to *have a realistic time line* for the research and show that you know what order you will do it in.

- Believe it or not, the hard conceptual work also includes the *project title and abstract or summary*. These have to get to the heart of the project in very few words. Doing it well is an art form. When an assessor is reading your bid these are what they will usually come to first. The title and the abstract are like a newspaper headline and strap line in the sense that they try to compress meaning but at the same time grab attention. They are also often the public face of the project, so they can't be full of in-house language that the informed lay person can't even begin to comprehend. We think your abstract should try for a 'killer ending' which points to the significance of the research and lingers in the mind.

What ultimately gives your bid the winning edge in highly competitive sponsored research funding fields? This is a very difficult question to answer because frankly it is often an indefinable quality that makes the bid sparkle. 'Innovation' is the common buzz word but it fails to capture what we are talking about. The ideas in a winning bid sing; they intrigue, enliven and excite the reader. They have a wow! factor. Ultimately they will generate in the academic peer reviewer a genuine desire to see the finished product when the project is over. Many good solid and technically competent pieces of research do get funded, no doubt, but the proposals that have this sort of compelling edge go to the top of the pile.

If you are seeking to win a contract research grant the chances are you that will be assessed by a committee formed by the funding body. This may include some of your academic peers but is unlikely to be dominated either numerically or, indeed, ideologically by them. This is not to say that the committee has no experience of research. It is probable that it includes people from within the funding body who have research expertise both in terms of their qualifications and in terms of the work they do for the organisation. Trusts and foundations are likely to obtain academic referees' reports that they will consider in their decision-making processes.

The likelihood also exists that the research project's focus has been clearly established and also much of its broad design. In that case, you will need to undertake rather different intellectual work from that outlined above. Or, to put it another way, the things outlined above will have a somewhat different inflection.

You will still need to show a number of things:

- You have *a strong knowledge of the main debates and issues in the field*. However, the debates in the research literature may not be as pertinent as those within which the funder is immersed. The funder's priorities as outlined on its website and the specifications of the actual research project will make these pretty clear. In very broad terms, such debates are usually associated with various sorts of practice, with on-the-ground problems or with 'out there among the public' issues that are making politicians' lives difficult. Youth suicide, for instance, or global warming, or terrorism, or family law, or drugs.

- You need to show that you have *a strong knowledge of the research methods involved*. However, it is unlikely that you will be expected to problematise them unless that is part of the project brief. It is much more likely that you will have to demonstrate to the committee that you are an expert in the application of the method and can deliver clear and convincing results through its application to the research question, problem or issue.

  As you know, sponsored research may be associated with commercialisation; that is, making money from the research outputs and applications. If this is the case, you need to demonstrate knowledge of the path that your research will take to commercial development in the market place – the so-called 'path to market'.

- You will need to persuasively demonstrate *the relevance and reliability of your track record;* that your team is outstanding and the best one for the job. The track record that is best valued in relation to contract research is not necessarily that most valued by your academic peers. Most contract research has an applied, action or change orientation. The selection committee is likely to want to see that you have a record of or at least a strong interest in such things. So it is important for you to be able to show that you are more than 'just an academic expert' unfamiliar with the ways of the world, full of airy-fairy, highfalutin' ideas relevant only to the ivory tower. You know the stereotypes often traded here and, unfortunately, you do need to understand that they are sometimes in the minds of members of funding committees. You must knock such stereotypes on the head with regard to your funding application and your research team. This is not the place for obscurantism or intellectual posturing – but is there ever really a place for that even in the academy?

So what are some of the key differences between sponsored and contract research and what are the implications for the conceptual work you will have to do?

- In contract research, the research questions, methods, time-lines, 'deliverables' (outcomes, outputs) are likely to be more closely specified by the funder than in sponsored research.

- You probably will not have to be as overtly concerned with theory as you would be in a sponsored project. The theory will often be implicit and undeclared and you will not be expected to problematise it. You may, however, be expected to subscribe to the funder's implicit theories in your application, at least in the first instance, and probably throughout the project. Indeed, if you problematise the funder's theory in the application it is likely to be the kiss of death. Let us be blunt here. If you can't stand the theory, don't do the bid. Simple. If you do, it will only cause you heartache. At least, that is our view, but others say: get in there, get your hands dirty, if you don't do the bid someone worse than you will, and then where will the world be? They try to see the good sense in the project, to maximise it in their research and project reports and to minimise the bad sense. Perversely, we are sympathetic to this argument too.

A trade secret. We should let you in on a secret at this point. People in government departments do not necessarily hold the views of their political 'masters'. So, although they may put the project specifications together in such a way as to satisfy and gratify their bosses, they may also try to leave them open to interpretation and open for the researcher to come in with a somewhat different take. Indeed, there may be a 'hidden text' associated with the bid which is not known to you. If you have good networks within the funding institution you may be able to informally get access to this. Having done so you may find that you need to write your bid with a hidden text also. Again, your conceptual and creative skills will need to be mobilised so that you get the right blend of commitment to the project with a tiny hint of scepticism.

- Contract research may be highly charged politically – particularly if you are doing it for government. The focus and the output may be controversial and may propel your reports and you into protracted negotiations with your 'project management team' appointed by the funder – though you might have a say in who is on it. They may not like what you do and want you to change your report, or bury the report and you.

What has politics got to do with winning bids? Some academics claim to have no position; no stand point. They say that they can take on any project in a dispassionate and disinterested fashion and deliver as the project specifications indicate. This no-stance stance means that they are tame pussycats and often win grants because of this. Of course their no-stance is total nonsense as their actual standpoint is usually purely instrumental. Their aim is to secure grants and all the accompanying kudos and power/knowledge, no matter what. Now, you can be a tame pussycat if you wish and yes, it will allow you to win some grants in the short term. However, if you get this sort of reputation your credibility as an expert will diminish and in the end you will not win the grants. This is because a hired gun (to mix the metaphors) must not be seen as a hired gun but rather as a dispassionate and disinterested expert. It is an interesting paradox is it not?

It is possible to infer from much of what we have said thus far that contract research is pretty one-sided and that for you there is little opportunity for agenda setting. Certainly winning such grants usually means putting in applications that stick closely to the specifications but it also involves enriching them. Enrichment does not mean adding new directions or issues, or taking the bid off in new directions. It means that, in the terms of the tender, you make it clear you are not only 'across the issues' but also have a depth that may not be of the sort that the funder's people have. Keep in mind here that those who developed the project or tender specifications and are assessing your application will often have expertise that they want enriched but they also want to fund someone who is in sympathy with the agenda which informs the tender. Winning thus means establishing your credibility and compatibility on the topic but also your capacity to 'add value'. And you must also establish your credibility as someone, or as a team, who will deliver promptly and in a way that is of practical use. This notion of enrichment suggests that researchers can often interpret the project rather more liberally than may at first appear possible and they may thus help to shape agendas.

And the winner is ...

What ultimately gives your bid the winning edge in highly competitive contract research funding fields? Again, this is hard to specify, partly because such fields are so diverse and involve many different value systems with regard to knowledge production, circulation and consumption. Maybe the secret is about understanding the value systems that are peculiar to the specific funding body and ensuring that your bid speaks to those values while at the same time enriching them. We are not sure. Again, though, we think the wow factor comes into play, although this time the wow is associated with the potential the bid appears to offer for addressing the priorities and needs of the funder.

Dealing with time, timetables and reporting requirements

Some project briefs set the time-lines up for you, in others you are free to set up your own and in yet others the broad parameters are set and you will devise more specific time lines within them. In *Getting Started on Research* we talk about phases and deadlines and offer an example of a time-line. Let us consider these issues a little more now in the light of the imperative to win grants from funding bodies.

Even though some funders do not set time-lines you do need to know what length of project they are prepared to support. Such matters will usually be laid out on their website. And you can go back through the records to see what is typically funded. A core part of developing your project is deciding on its length. Is it a short pilot project? Is it a longitudinal study that may require several rounds of funding over the years? But beyond these obvious differences, how do you work out how long your project is to be? The length you finally decide on will be a judicious combination of what the funder is prepared to pay for and what you are trying to do. Many people start with the specified or average time that a funder provides funding for and then work their projects into that time frame. They modify the project's questions, purposes, activities and outcomes accordingly. As always, some try to fudge things and others have a totally unrealistic notion of what is possible. Indeed, there is a tendency among academics to promise much more than can be delivered and to deliver more than is paid for.

Usually it is obvious to the funder, if, for example, it is a project that really requires only one year's funding but you are trying to string it out to three and get three years' funding. And project bids that claim that the researchers will do what is patently impossible do not get funded. Some mistakenly think that funders see such projects as value for

TABLE 3   Overall research plan: timetable of activities in different locations over three years

Year	Sem.	Location	Activity
2002	1	UniSA	Establishment stage – apply for ethics clearance and employ research assistant
		Interstate	Build policy archive and begin analysis Conduct and analyse interviews with policy agents in Australia (twenty-four) Select six university cameo studies in SA, Vic and NSW
	2	UniSA	Continue policy text analysis
		Interstate	Conduct and analyse university sector cameo studies Select six school cameo studies in SA, Vic and NSW
2003	1	UniSA	Intertextual analysis of policy texts
		Interstate	Conduct and analyse school cameo studies Prepare for international interviews Select six VET case studies in SA, Vic and NSW
	2	Overseas	Conduct and analyse international interviews (eighteen)
		Interstate	Conduct and analyse VET cameo studies Select six informal education settings for cameos in SA, Vic and NSW
2004	1	Interstate UniSA	Conduct cameo studies of informal education settings in SA, Vic and NSW Begin synthesis of material for book
	2	UniSA	Write book

money. They are usually seen as rather foolish. So asking the answerable question and developing the do-able project is crucially tied up with getting the timing right.

Similar points apply to the milestones of the project. In much contract research these are specified at the start and are monitored. What you submit to your funder is sometimes called a deliverable. It may, for example, be a literature review to be submitted after the first three months, then a set of case studies in the second three months and so on. Some funders will not advance the next lot of money until the previous deliverable is in and approved.

In sponsored research you usually establish your own milestones, and your funding application will clearly lay them out. How you organise your time is up to you but we find it handy to do it by university semesters. Table 3 is an example of one of Jane's grants organised in this way. It is from her Australian Research Council project called *Knowledge/economy/society: a sociological study of an education policy discourse in Australia in globalising circumstances*. There are several things for novices to notice about this timetable:

- It includes an establishment phase.
- Each stage anticipates the next.
- The analysis of the data is built in at the various stages.
- The main publication is included in the time line.

We cannot overemphasise the importance of including everything in the timetable, and note that Jane might also have included conference presentations and other publications. The broad point is to plan a publishing schedule early and to avoid project debt.

Project debt

Many researchers, new and old, fall into the trap of gathering and analysing data right up to the end of the funding period. What often happens then is that they roll on to another project and do the same thing all over again, moving into a state of constant 'debt' to earlier projects. Sometimes it becomes impossible for them to repay the debts and half-written papers and chapters languish in the bottom of filing cabinets alongside boxes and boxes of unanalysed data. This does not look good when it comes time to do the final project report. And, even if you repay the project debt later your final report will be a record which indicates that the project did not produce the goods. Your reputation among those who distribute research funds is thus diminished and you may become known as someone who does not deliver.

Most projects require *interim and end of award reports*. The structure of these is often set out by the funder. You are usually expected to explain:

- Whether the project has altered from the original and in what ways. These may have to be approved.

- Whether the project is going to plan.
- What your preliminary or concluding results are or what you have achieved.
- Whether you have experienced any difficulties that affected the progress of the research project.
- What your research plans and objectives are for the coming year.
- Your outputs to date.

With the intensified emphasis on the accountability for research funding and on 'impact' particular attention is paid to your outputs. Table 4 shows the form that the Australian Research Council asks researchers to use in reporting the project's 'academic outputs'. You can check out the funding council in your own country to see how it expects you to report.

You should note that researchers are asked not to include 'forthcoming' and 'submitted' work. So those half-finished papers and the debt you have accumulated from previous projects simply don't count. As you see, many outputs are covered in this form. Increasingly funders are looking for other indices of impact, including press coverage and citations. Witness this, also from the ARC.

- *Evidence of scholarly impact and contribution.* Is there evidence that this research project is having/has had an impact in the research field or the broader public domain? If yes, give details.

The ARC has access to standard citation data on articles published in ISI journals. However, there may be other indicators of impact including, for example, citations to books, republication, translations, reviews, invited keynote addresses, other invitations, newspaper/ media/expert commentary.

- *Research commercialisation.* If there has been commercialisation resulting from the research project, in the period covered by this report, give details.

In the case of the ARC these reports are not published. But different systems do things differently, of course, and some expect much more substantial reports which must be publicly available, and these may even be peer-reviewed or subject to some kind of evaluation. In the case of contract research normally a publishable report is required at the end of the project, sometimes including recommendations.

TABLE 4   Form from the Australian Research Council

Publications and other academic outputs. Enter the number of publications in each category, for the period covered by this report. Where appropriate, enter full publication details; include 'published' and 'in press' publications but exclude 'forthcoming' and 'submitted' work.

Item	Category	Number	Publication details
A1	Book – authored research		
A2	Book – authored other		
A3	Book – edited		
A4	Book – revision/new edition		
A5	Book – translation		
B	Book chapter		
C1	Journal article – articles in scholarly refereed journal		
C2	Journal article – other contribution to refereed journal		
C3	Journal article – non-refereed article		
C4	Journal articles – letter or note		
D	Major reviews		
E1	Conference – full written paper – refereed proceedings		
E2	Conference – full written paper – non-refereed proceedings		
E3	Conference – extract of paper		
E4	Conference – edited volume of conference proceedings		
E5	Conference – unpublished presentation		
F	Audio-visual recording		
G	Computer software		
H	Designs		
J1	Major creative works		
J2	Creative work included in group exhibition, performance, recording or anthology		
J3	Exhibition curatorship		
K	Other academic outputs (in categories other than those above)		

Doing the budget

You *must* read the rules and apply only for money for the kinds of things that the funder will pay for. Don't include anything else, because if you do it will be clear that you have not read the rules or that you are 'trying it on'. Given the university imperative to bring in the bucks, you are under inexorable pressure to win grants. This may lead you to bid low; in other words, not to charge the full costs of the project and to ask for less money/time than you need. Universities, however, expect full cost recovery and you must not under-sell yourself. This will come back to bite you, big time, if you do.

You may be able to apply for money for:

- Salaries (research assistance, secretarial and administrative support).
- Teaching release (possibly all or part of your own).
- Equipment (computers, tape recorders, digital cameras).
- Consumables (software, video and audio-tapes).
- Books.
- Maintenance or overheads, including phone, printing, office expenses, photocopying, library requests, postage.
- Travel to research sites and conferences and associated *per diem* expenses.
- Payments to respondents and respondents' expenses.
- Payments to a project consultancy group or for individual consultancies.
- The costs of advertising for staff.
- Printing and dissemination costs, including the possibility of payments to commercial publishers or submission charges by certain journals.
- Some funding bodies will also pay for the cost of developing the grant. Indeed, when thinking about costings, bear in mind that one of the costs you have to cover is the cost of getting the grant in the first place.

You may be asked to indicate items in order of priority. If you are working across institutions you must indicate how the money will be divided between you. Make sure that resources (financial and other) are equitably distributed within the team, or if not, that the team has agreed to this.

Your university will have lists of pay scales for all the staff you wish to employ – casual (by the hour) or contract (by the calendar time period) and by levels of seniority based on experience. And you will have to consider carefully the levels of expertise you want, can afford and can convincingly justify to the funder. With salaries, always include 'on costs': leave loadings, salary increments and any other predicted extra costs. These vary according to the type and length of employment and can have quite an effect on your budget. You also have to find a balance between what is in the best interests of the project and what is in the best interests of the people you employ. Hopefully these coincide, but sometimes not. We try to keep our staff happy first, as it is best for them and also for the project. If you are seeking funding for an extended period you should factor in likely cost rises (e.g. airline costs). Make sure you have factored in sufficient clerical and administrative support and that you have distinguished it from your research assistance. You do not want to be doing the clerical work yourself and neither is it necessarily appropriate for your RA to be doing it.

In developing your budget you also need to find out certain things from your university, above and beyond the question of salary scales. Issues that arise regularly with regard to budgets are as follows:

- Who is available to help me do my budget? You will find that the university has all manner of people who may be available to help you at the various stages of doing your budget. These include business or financial managers; research officers, budget officers, 'human resources' staff. Make full use of them early. Once your budget is complete you will be expected to have it officially checked by one or other of these people to make sure all costs have been factored in at the right rates.

- What percentage of the budget do you need to allocate to cover university overheads? Most universities will charge a standard fee but you may also find that structures further down the university food chain also charge, for instance your school or faculty. Your dean or equivalent manager will not sign off on projects until these costs are built into the budget. You need to find out what the project gets for such a percentage. Usually it covers such things as the management, administrative and advice systems set up to support research but also includes such basic things as the use of offices, existing equipment and lighting and so forth. It does not usually include phone use, fax, photocopying costs and the like.

- You should discuss with your head of school the time you need for the project, whether they are prepared to release you from other duties to allow for it, the space that is available for your new research staff, whether you actually need to buy new computers and other equipment or whether there might be some available that can be used, university or other funds that may be available if the funder is seeking co-funding. In other words you need to know the institutional resources that are available for the research. And, while you have their attention, you should find out what research staff they know of who might be available for the project and how good they are.

- How do you pay the university for the time you spend on the project and at what rates? Because most universities are less and less funded to undertake research out of government block grants they now expect users to pay for every aspect of the research project. This includes your time. You need to talk to your head of school or dean about this. You may be expected to charge your full replacement cost or you may just be expected to charge for teaching replacement. This is usually at your current salary level even if someone at a level lower replaces you. There are some exceptions. For instance, in Australia the Australian Research Council allocates institutions additional money when academics win ARC project grants. This means staff do not have to include the cost of their own time in the grant application.

Your budget will be carefully checked by the funder and by its peer reviewers. They will be asked to see where your budget can be cut. You will usually be required to include a budget justification, which is designed to assist them make such judgements. You will often find the budget cut no matter how good the justification. We have included quite a detailed budget justification below so that you can see the sorts of things you need to do. It is from Jane's ARC *Knowledge economy* project mentioned above. We might add that despite the following details the budget was cut.

C2 Justification of funding requested from the ARC

The direct costs requested from the ARC for this project per year averages at $57 820 per annum.

Personnel

A research assistant (RA, level 5–7, over three years) will be appointed at 0.6 fraction, three months into the project. The level of appointment reflects the high level of responsibility the RA will assume in working closely with the CI throughout the project. The appointee will be required to possess highly advanced research, critical and communication skills. The RA will be responsible for the creation of a policy archive in the first year and as he/she will be subsequently involved in the analysis of policy documents and other data, a knowledge of theory is required. The RA will assist in conducting interviews for the cameo studies and in writing the proposed book and papers. A secretarial assistant (general staff, level 4, step 3) will be employed casually. The level of appointment is based on the need for an experienced person able to complete tasks with a minimum of supervision. Further, as transcription will make up a large component of their duties, efficient and accurate audio-typing skills are imperative. The anticipated number of hours of transcription has been calculated using the number of hours of interviews each year (sixty-six hours in year 1, 102 hours in year 2, and forty-two hours in year 3), multiplied by three hours of transcription per hour of taped interview. The cost of additional administrative assistance for years 1–3 of the project (fifty hours, 100 hours and fifty hours, respectively) has been added. The secretarial assistant will be responsible for scheduling interviews and making travel arrangements for the CI. He/she will also give general administrative support (photocopying, faxing and correspondence). The budgeted salaries include on costs, leave loading and annual increments for the RA and 20 per cent casual loading for the secretarial assistant. Both take into account enterprise bargaining rises.

▶ ## *Teaching relief*

Teaching relief of twenty-four days is requested for the final semester of the project in order to provide free time for the CI to focus fully on writing the proposed book. Teaching relief will expedite delivery to the publisher and, thus, the dissemination of the research results. The requested amount is calculated using the base rate of the ARC Senior Research Associate scale.

Maintenance

Good-quality recording equipment is required to record interviews, including an omnidirectional flat microphone. This will be required for both the CI and the RA, as the RA will conduct VET cameo studies while the CI is interviewing overseas. The budget for audio-tapes reflects the need to retain primary data. It is anticipated that the bulk of the money requested for maintenance will be spent on telephone and photocopying costs. Although the university will provide for reasonable photocopying and phone costs, these expenses will be larger than average. The creation of a policy archive will lead to large amounts of printing and photocopying as well as library costs, particularly in year 1. Telephone budget estimates are based on the anticipated expense of negotiating interviews with inter-state and international agencies and senior staff and phone interviews with participants both preceding and following each cameo study and set of interviews with policy agents. Data collection is concentrated in the second year and includes international telephone calls in addition to STD expenses. This is reflected in the amount requested in the second year.

Travel

This project aims to amass data from state, national and international sources, and this is reflected in the travel budget. Private car reimbursement is requested for cameo studies and state government interviews conducted in South Australia, and five-day advance ▶

▶   booking air fares, *per diems* and local transport costs for Victoria and New South Wales. Travel will occur according to the project's overall design, with studies conducted at a rate of one sector per semester. Within this constraint, travel costs have been kept to an absolute minimum and, in order to reduce air fares, the two cameo studies per sector per state in semesters 2–5 will be conducted during the one visit. Overseas interviews will be conducted with senior staff in: Paris (UNESCO and OECD); Brussels (Education International and EU); Geneva (ILO); and Washington DC (World Bank). The budget includes a round-the-world air ticket. Overseas *per diems* and local transport have been determined with regard to the current value of the Australian dollar.

What happens next?

It depends, yet again, on the funder.

- If you have put in an expression of interest, you may get a letter asking for a full application.
- You may be asked by the potential funder to provide more detail or to come for an interview.
- You may get the reviewers' reports and be asked to respond. If you do, take this very seriously and get advice about how best to do it.

Whatever the case you are in limbo till the results emerge. But do you sit on your hands till then? No, for you still have your funding calendar, which tells you which you-friendly grant possibilities are coming up, and you know that there are regular opportunities that will always be there. Now is when you take the bid you have developed and see what other sources of money may be available to support all or part of it. Also, consider the possibility of doing a little unfunded research in relation to it – a pilot study or needs assessment, for instance. Or perhaps in putting the bid together you spotted some serious holes in your CV or your researcher identity. Consider attending to these. You may, for example, have some conference papers that need to be written up or some data from a previous project that is not yet analysed and written up. Or you may just have recognised that you need to do some more reading. Whatever you do, don't imagine that once the bid is in you can rest on your laurels, fabulous though they may be.

And what if you hear you have missed out? Damn! Damn! Damn! Quite naturally you will feel disappointed and possibly inadequate. You may also feel annoyed with the funders, the reviewers (what do they know?) or your university for pushing you to chase research dollars. You may be jealous of your successful colleagues. You may conclude that you will never be a researcher and decide to chuck it all in. You may become cynical about the whole damn research enterprise. We have all been there, done that, and it sucks. However, you do have to get over it, and the sooner the better. A few nights of bitter and twisted invective shared with a sympathetic colleague and accompanied by whatever comforts you best are okay. But several weeks? Nah! As soon as you can bring yourself to, have a chat with your mentors and your best academic colleagues and get back to your research agenda. No-one wins all the time and everyone must expect to rework applications for subsequent funding rounds or other possible funders. And on no account should you ignore the feedback which led your bid to fall over. Use that and other feedback to rewrite your bid.

This has been a detailed and complex chapter, and for good reason, as the outline of the various tasks involved in writing a winning research application indicates. As we have shown, writers of winning bids know that it is a game about horses for courses.

Project Management

In this chapter we talk you through the project establishment stage and the issues you will deal with as the project proceeds, including working in a team, publishing and dissemination.

Where are you now?

At this point you have heard that you have won the bid. Wild celebrations are in order, of course. Winning is great, and you will be on a high for while, or maybe for the length of the project. But it is not uncommon for people to feel anxious at this stage, particularly if it is their first funded project. You may remember, for instance, all the things you promised – or foolishly over-promised. You may realise what a very hard slog it will be to complete the project and that there will be no relief for the next few years. You may wonder how it will be possible to do the project and all your other work. You may even panic, and with good reason if the research starts Monday next. Well, there is no escaping. You won the money, now you have to do the work. Our task in this chapter is to give you some tips on managing the project well, with the least possible trauma and the best possible results.

The establishment stage

The contract

The contract will accompany any offer of an external funding grant and you must deal with it pronto. It may come with the letter of offer or it may arise after a period of discussion and negotiation with the funder. If the contract is from a funding body such as a research council it will be standard and you can comfortably sign it and your university will do the rest. For other grants you must have your university's legal adviser take a look and help you negotiate any necessary changes. If you are working across several universities each university's legal adviser will have to check it, especially if the money is to go to the separate institutions rather than through one lead university. Prior to doing this, you must check it to see if everything is there and that nothing has changed or been slipped in under your guard. Major matters of concern are time-lines, deliverables and intellectual property.

Also you must attend to things that have changed since you put in the bid. Perhaps the original time-lines have become difficult or the project team may have altered. Under such circumstances the contract needs to be changed and you, or the solicitor, must negotiate this with the funder. Make sure that you can still meet time-lines and that they include everything, particularly the work of the final project stages. Do not get caught doing final revisions to reports after the project is complete and payment over. Funders will vary on the amount of time that is seen as acceptable or necessary between the offering and the signing of the contract and indeed the end of the project and the final report. For instance, the ESRC in the UK insists on a six-week gap between the offer and the signing, and all reports must be submitted three months after the project finishes.

We discuss Intellectual Property Rights (IPR) at length in *Writing for Publication*. In this context you need to think about how to deal with IPR provision in research contracts and make sure it is not only clear from the beginning but does what you want. Don't sign away your right to be known as the researchers and to publish from the project. What you want is the right to:

- Have your team's name and institutions on all the project publications put out by the funder.
- Publish from the project in peer-refereed journals.
- Talk publicly about the project outcomes to your colleagues and the media. You do not want to be gagged for ever – but you may be happy to be gagged for a while to give your funder a chance to read and think about your report.
- Publish the report yourself if the funder refuses to publish it for whatever reason.
- Royalties and other copyright money.

Melissa has done heaps of research and development projects for government education systems. They have involved producing innumerable curriculum and other documents and reports either alone or in teams. She has a fine mind and some astute, practical and original ideas. She also works hard, and in fact usually does most of the work despite being a member of a team. Almost invariably the good ideas are hers. In her early days of doing such government work she was quite naive about matters of IPR. Although she produced a huge amount of curriculum material little had her name on it. Of course this is not unusual in government circles. It did not particularly worry her until she found quite a bit of her work put out under someone else's name. Subsequently she has been much smarter about IPR. Indeed, she recently had a financial windfall from the Australian copyright agency.

Doing budget and project revisions

You don't always get all the money you asked for despite your carefully crafted and totally persuasive budget justifications. Once you know your final amount you must carefully revise your budget for the entire period of the project. This will require you to revise aspects of the project. You cannot try to deliver what you have not been funded for. So downsize your activities and promises and revise your time-line and publishing plan if necessary. Before doing so check to see if your institution can provide you with any top-up money – you may get lucky.

Finding and appointing your research staff

Employ your research and other support staff early. While you can't make or finalise appointments before your contract is through and your budget revised, there are things you can do in advance.

- *Keep your eye open for good people.* Let your colleagues know you need research and/or administrative assistants. They may be able to recommend people to you – but don't just take their word for it. Check out the work of anyone recommended if you can, and do not promise anything until you are in a position to. If you can appoint someone good without going to external advertisement, this is a bonus, as it saves time and money. But it may also mean you do not get the best person. Don't be too hasty to appoint someone just because they are there, warm and upright. You also need to be careful that you don't fall foul of equal opportunities principles and regulations.

- *If you have to advertise*, chat to people in your human resources (personnel) division to see what it entails, how much it costs, and consider what the project can afford now your budget has been revised.

- *Write a preliminary advertisement and job description.* Consider carefully the selection criteria, job description and application time-lines. The personnel people may be able help you do this. Think about who you want to have on the selection committee and line them up informally.

- *Line up all the necessaries* – office and desk space, computers, access keys, telephone access and the like – so that once someone is on board they can get down to work immediately. If you are in a research group or centre, there may be people available to help you do this.

Appointing people is just the start of what you need to do. Once you have them on board you will have to:

- Make sure they have a thorough induction into all those aspects of the university that are pertinent to the project. For example, have them spend some time on the Web getting to know research policies and procedures and in the library, introduce them to the university's email and other systems, and to other researchers, research support staff and research leaders.

- Sit down with them and carefully go though the project, noting particularly time-lines and deadlines. Make sure they understand the project's purposes and the expected outputs.

- Clarify their working hours, role and responsibilities. Make clear what you expect of them and that they are responsible to you.

- Let them know they must plan their holidays and include them within the time of the contract.

- Clarify questions of authorship and ownership with them early. Indicate whether these are negotiable and on what grounds.

- In the context of the time-line, set them to work on a small set of activities, which can be evaluated at the end of that time. Keep a close eye on their work.

- If research assistants are doing research degrees within the project, factor in the fact that they have to be able to identify what work is theirs to legitimately claim their PhD. This is quite difficult and requires very careful and sensitive negotiation and monitoring. Lifelong enmities have arisen out of failure to clarify who owns what under such circumstances.

Today, Daniel and Don are both big guns in their field. They both have Chairs. In earlier times, though, Daniel was Don's PhD supervisor. In fact he recruited Don to work with him on a funded project. For a while they got on really well and the relationship was highly generative for both of them. However, as time went on the relationship became more rivalrous. Daniel started to assert his seniority and to claim many of Don's insights for the project. Don was incensed and tried to secure them for his PhD, even going so far as to take the case further up the university system. The rivalry had initially been contained within the project team but now it was public knowledge. Eventually it was resolved, but the deep hostilities remained and sadly spilled over into subsequent workplaces and professional relationships. People were 'recruited' either to Don's or to Daniel's team. Many colleagues did not want to take sides, as they found the whole thing distasteful.

Applying for ethics approval

If you are doing research with people (often and insultingly referred as 'human subjects') or animals you must get ethics approval from your university and possibly other research sites before you commence your research. You need to find out what the requirements are in your particular situation. In many countries and universities this should be done before submitting your grant application to the funding agency. In others, the university will only be willing to consider ethics approval once the grant is obtained. Whatever, you should already have thought about the ethical dimensions of your research when writing the research proposal, and you can find out more about this in *Getting Started on Research*.

Your university website will probably have all the details and forms on line and will also have the dates of ethics committee meetings. You may also need ethics approval from your other research sites. If you are doing research in medical settings getting ethics approval may be particularly onerous. If you haven't had to get ethics approval before-hand and you have been able to appoint a research assistant, then tracking down what you need to do in this respect is a good early job for them, as is working on early drafts of your various ethics applications. Some institutions will require you to renew your ethics approval annually – and if your project has changed you may even need to apply afresh. At the end of the project, your university may also require a final ethics report.

University ethics committees tend to be very determined and cautious, always want their instructions followed to the letter and also prefer more rather than less detail. The more you give them first up the more likely is their quick approval. They are also very conservative and don't take kindly to methodological innovation or 'out there' topics. If your project fits these descriptions put a great deal of extra care into your ethics application, carefully and convincingly laying out your legitimations and justifications.

Your publishing and dissemination plan

Authorship and attribution are among the most contentious aspects of team research. Recognise this up front and deal with it. Reach an agreement and put it in writing. The sorts of things you will need to negotiate are as follows: How the publications will be authored. Will all team members' names be on each paper? If so, in what order? How will book authorship be ordered, alphabetically or in order of contribution? How is 'contribution' to be understood? What if you do not want your name on a certain paper? Of course you have that right, but what does it do for team morale? Is having single or sub-group-authored papers the best way to go, provided they always acknowledge the project and the rest of the project team in footnotes? If so, what are your responsibilities with regard to critical feedback on others' drafts? At what point does heaps and heaps of feedback turn into at least associate authorship? Are you better-off negotiating authorship on a case-by-case basis? We have tried various methods. None is perfect and you can get stung in many unexpected ways. Don't ask us to elaborate! The main thing is to agree and to keep the lines of communication open on the topic. If the approach you agreed on does not appear to be working, talk about it and renegotiate it. Don't brood, it's an awful waste of energy.

The on-going work

Looking after your budget

You have your revised budget and you are now spending money on staff, various sorts of infrastructure and travel. Here are the questions you need answered about the university's finance practices with regard to research money:

- Can you get a credit card for your research project?
- What do you do with receipts for costs incurred outside the university? Indeed, do you have a decent system for keeping receipts?
- What can you sign off on?
- Can you, should you, keep your own accounts and records? How is this best done?
- How can you keep a check on your accounts?
- How does the university keep you informed of your expenditure?
- Can you understand the forms they send you? These are usually in totally incomprehensible codes and are organised in counter-intuitive ways.

Most early career researchers don't know the answers to these questions. However, some universities do run short training sessions on the university's finance systems and the software packages used and it very useful to go along to these so you can get up to speed quickly. If your university does not offer such things suggest to your research office that they offer them as a research training activity for new researchers. Such activity should include preparing budgets, using spreadsheets and the like. If no formal training exists, or if you have done the training and still don't understand, it may be worth going to see your finance officer and asking her or him to explain the budgeting systems to you. Not only can you ask the questions you need answered, but it will also mean that the finance officer is more likely to remember you and respond quickly to your questions in future.

You must never ever put your trust in the university to keep your records correctly and thus pass all responsibility over to it. Mistakes are always made with mysterious outgoings and incomings. You must regularly check your budgets and fix them up pronto.

Leadership and membership of research teams

The research team is central to the success of the project. It is crucial that you get your membership and leadership right. A good research team is hugely productive in many ways and is a joy to be part of. We have each been blessed on many occasions in this regard. However, we have also had some less than pleasant and productive experiences. These drag you and the research down. If you have appointed good research staff that is a good start. Research teams include the following combinations:

- The sole grant winner and:
  - Research staff.
  - Research staff and a PhD student and/or a postdoctoral appointment.
  - A project consultancy or management team invited and appointed by the grant winner or by the funder.
- A grant-winning team consisting mainly of:
  - Academics at one university or more, within one or more school, department, research centre or discipline, within one or more state or country, and research staff.
  - Research staff and a PhD student and/or a postdoctoral appointment.
  - A project consultancy or management team invited and appointed by the grant winner or by the funder.
- A grant-winning team consisting of academics and research partners from elsewhere: industry, government, the community, the profession, anywhere. This team might include any or all the above and also:
  - Research staff appointed by the partner.
  - Permanent employees of the partner whose work has been diverted to the project either part or full time.

Teams are complex and consist of many types of research identities and relationships. Team members might include very experienced researchers and novices, people with different types of research experience and with different expectations of the project's processes and outcomes.

Handy hints about team work

Being the boss. Almost inevitably teams involve some sort of formal and clear power hierarchy. Certain people are the employing researchers and others are the research workers employed on a contract and answerable to you, the boss. Being the boss does not mean being tyrannical, exploitative or a dragon of the first order. Neither does it mean becoming your staff's new best friend or their therapist, life coach or mother/father figure. It does mean taking responsibility for the work and working conditions of your employees and treating your staff with respect and care. At a minimum your role is to:

- Clearly allocate, schedule and oversee their work.
- Make sure it gets done.
- Evaluate it and assist them to improve it if necessary.
- Ensure that the conditions in which they undertake that work are conducive to working well, and are safe and healthy.
- Know the rules and procedures that govern employment in your university.

You are a *really* good boss if you do such things as:

- Give lots of feedback to your researchers about when their work is going well and how it might be improved.
- Get them to talk about how they think they are going and what might help them to work better.
- Find out if they need any additional training and organise that for them. Perhaps plan a programme for their time of employment with you.
- Keep in mind that they also have a future and consider how their involvement in the project might help them in their own career plans.
- Factor into their work any rewards that you can which will increase their enjoyment of their work and their attachment to the project.
- See your role as offering research training for your research staff and give them plenty of opportunities to build their skills through new research-related experiences.
- Help them gain new positions and/or develop their own projects as their work on yours draws to a close.

Researcher/contract researcher relationships can get difficult if, for instance, the contract researcher is your PhD student, long-standing friend, lover, a member of your family, your daughter's best friend or whatever. Such complicated relationships are best avoided in our view. But relationships can get difficult anyway. And, of course, you may become friendly with your research staff, occasions may require that you hear their personal troubles and take into account what is going on in their personal life. But ultimately they work for you and you are together to get a job of work done under the terms of the project and their employment contract. This is the base line.

You are a problematic boss if you do not do the 'good boss' things noted above, and if you:

- Don't do what you say you will.
- Are difficult to contact and talk with.
- Keep changing your mind or their schedule.
- Are rigid and don't allow a little flexibility when it is required.
- Expect them to work above or below their job descriptions and skills.
- Expect them to work above and beyond their paid working hours.
- Don't trust them to do the right thing by you.
- Do not properly acknowledge their work, or if you claim theirs as your own, failing to include their name on the paper. Some scoundrels do this and should be shot at dawn for it. It is not on. Paying someone for their work doesn't absolve you of your moral obligation for proper acknowledgement and attribution of their contributions.
- Do not consider their career development needs and help them move on from their position as your research assistant.

You, as boss, may have problems with your research staff if they:

- Do not listen.
- Do not do as they are asked.
- Are not up to the job and more training won't get them there in the short term.
- Skive off when they are supposed to be working.
- Turn up late for meetings.
- Try to take control of the project. Some like to call this 'managing up'. In some senses your researchers will have to do it when trying

to arrange aspects of the project or trying, for instance, to organise meetings. But we are talking here about when they try to make the sorts of decisions that are rightly yours and when they will not follow your instructions to do otherwise.

- Become possessive about project data, such as field notes, regarding it as their own rather than the project team's.
- Decide what they will do at their own rather than the project's convenience.
- Expect attributions or authorships that are beyond the level of their contribution. This happens quite often, and for some clarity about who has the right to be named as an author you can read *Writing for Publication.*
- Or if you end up doing the work they are supposed to be doing or having to double-check everything they have done because you do not trust them to do it properly.

You should know that sometimes any or all such problems may arise no matter how good a boss you are. While some RAs are bliss, some are hopeless.

Dealing with problems

There are no hard-and-fast rules for dealing with these two sets of problems except that they must be nipped in the bud early and you must take the lead in doing this. The first set of problems – about being a bad boss – is particularly difficult because your RA is unlikely to give you the feedback that will enable you to be a better boss. After all, there is an imbalance of power and you are not only the boss, you are also the source of future references, job opportunities and career sponsorship. The best thing you can do is: first follow the golden 'good boss' rules listed above, second make sure the lines of communication are as open and dialogical as possible and third regularly reflect critically and ruthlessly on your own boss practices.

The second set of problems – about having a poor RA – is not easy to deal with either, particularly if you are the sort of person who finds it difficult to be frank with people or who always makes excuses for them even when they are patently behaving inappropriately or if you compulsively avoid potentially conflictual or confrontational situations. Be clear on this. Such ways of being in the world do not help you, the project or indeed the contract researcher. You must name the problem and address it as soon as you are aware of it; don't indulge in avoidance strategies, otherwise known as the strategies of the totally gutless who cannot live up to their responsibilities to the project or the employee.

Your university's 'human resources' department will be able to provide you with advice and information about processes to follow. If the situation gets so bad that you have to sack the researcher you need to know what their and your legal rights are and you will need to have followed due process. This usually requires you to have clearly laid out your performance expectations for a set period and for the assistant's performance to be evaluated at the end of that period. It also involves a number of stages, and if they do not come up to scratch at the end of them you then have grounds for dismissal. This is a big step to take and hopefully it will not come to that.

Before entering the process you may try to deal with the recalcitrant staff member informally. There are a number of tactics you could try:

- Call a meeting and let the person know that you have concerns about their work and that you want to talk to them about the problem and how to resolve it quickly and without rancour.
- List your concerns and email your list to your researcher. Invite them to come to the meeting with an explanation and also with a set of propositions about how they might get up to speed.
- In the meeting first go though your concerns. Give them the chance to go though their responses to your concerns and to lay out any of their own. Quietly but firmly get them to agree that they must lift their game. (And, if you need to lift yours, then agree to do that too but do not take any blame where it is not warranted.) Go through their proposed ways of doing this. Share some of your own and let them know how you will monitor their work. Set out a time period for the first stage of this monitoring and let them know that if they are not up to speed, your next step is the formal university process.
- You must keep good, written records of all of this.

Louise was really rushed to appoint a research assistant on a new project of the 'starting Monday' variety. Jim worked down the corridor, seemed friendly and capable and had just finished his contract on another project. She got chatting to him at the photocopier ▶

▶ and before she knew it she was offering him the job – starting immediately. She did not have a chance to contact his previous employer until a few weeks into the project, at which time she learnt that he had been unsatisfactory and had actually been under a process of formal review. Louise had always been rather unimpressed with the previous employer and anyway thought that her superior people skills would ensure that Jim got up speed. Further, she had no time to follow though with the HR people to find out exactly what had happened and what it might mean for her work with Jim. As time went on she found that indeed Jim was below par and that he spent lots of time and effort trying to hide the fact. He took twice as long to do things as was reasonable but got defensive when she tried to 'intervene'. Meanwhile she found that she was regularly having to check his work, as she could never be sure that it would be done properly. When she had finally had enough and decided to institute a process of review herself, she found that she did not know how to go about it. By the time she found out, it became clear to her that she had no decent evidence of his poor work history because she herself had in fact covered over the trail. When she told him she intended nonetheless to institute proceedings, he was furious and complained about her to the union and senior staff. All this took huge amounts of time away from the project but she did not let the funder know of the problems she was having. Eventually a 'deliverable' was due that she could not deliver. The funder charged her a penalty from the next round of money she was due to get. When she protested, the funder pointed to the contract, which neither she nor the university solicitor had read before she signed it. She had no choice but to keep Jim on for the remainder of the project and to fund, out of another consultancy budget line, someone else to do his work.

Being a member of a collegial academic team

What of relationships within a project team consisting mainly of experienced or fledgling academics, including project PhD students and postdoctoral fellows (postdocs)? These need care too, especially when there are big differences of power and status.

Formal and informal lines of responsibility, authority and accountability

With the PhD students and the postdocs on your team it is likely you will also be their boss in that they were invited on to your project and thus work to you – although, as noted earlier, ownership of ideas and authorship of publications may be an issue. In such cases many of the points we made about being a good and very good boss apply. There may be chief and partner investigators on the team. Again it is clear that the responsibility for the project and the lines of authority within it are with the CIs. Also, if there is, or you are, a project director then the buck stops with them/you.

If you are all named on the project bid as CIs then it is open slather even if some team members are more junior than others. There are few guidelines even though this is the most common form of research practice. In such circumstances you would be well advised to attend to the following matters and to invent your own rules for the project no matter whether it is a long one or a short one.

Very early in the project negotiate *roles and responsibilities* and do up a responsibility matrix. We give an example of such a matrix in Table 5. You need to make sure that responsibilities are distributed equally and that no-one gets more to do than the others and that no-one gets more of the cream or the crap jobs than do others. However, too much democracy can be as problematic as too little. It is smart to make use of the particular skills people have. So, for instance, if one of the team is brilliant at statistics and the rest mediocre, it makes sense and is of overall benefit to the project if the stats person plays to their strengths. This may mean you do more menial things at some stages of the project. So what! There will be swings and roundabouts. On other occasions you may be doing the higher-order stuff while she is making the coffee. In other words, don't be too precious or too short-term in your thinking about team democracy. View project work in the whole and take things in the round. That said, more senior researchers have a responsibility to more junior colleagues to make sure that they are getting what they need out of a project and aren't being exploited by their ethically challenged colleagues and that they are not exploiting themselves. And the load will also be distributed according to role and level of responsibility.

TABLE 5   A responsibility matrix

Name	Role	Budget/ money	Talking to funder	Literature review and fieldwork	Data analysis	Writing
Jamila	Chief investigator	✓	✓	10%	Supervisory Keeping an overview	Lead role
Peter	Partner investigator			10%	Quantitative data	Quantitative aspects
Anne	Research associate			50% (and to help Ilan). Setting up access to research sites	Qualitative data	Support Jamila and Peter
Ilan	Part-time research assistant PT doctoral student			30% with special attention to the literature review	Support to Peter and Anne	

Ethical practice in research teams

Not all research bosses or general members of a research team are highly reflexive about their own practices and some have no clue. Sadly, also, some contract researchers or junior members of research teams do not even know when they are getting ripped off. You are being exploited if:

- You wrote or contributed significantly to the conceptualisation of the bid but you are not a co-applicant (unless it is your job specifically to be developing bids with and in support of other people).
- You are employed fractionally but are working much more than that.
- You are employed as a research assistant but you are doing the work of a more senior research associate.
- Your work on a project is not appropriately recognised or acknowledged, e.g. you did a substantial amount of analysis of quantitative data but that's not acknowledged.
- Someone else uses your ideas without acknowledgement.

When there is a project team consisting of a number of academics it is sometimes not made clear to the research support staff what the *lines of authority and accountability* are. How should they work to a team? How can you avoid giving them conflicting directives? It is beneficial all round if there are clear lines of accountability: who should they go to first, who should they go to for what? In the early stages of the project the academics on the team would be well advised to sort this out and to discuss together what it means to be good and very good bosses and then for the rest of the project to monitor their progress on it, perhaps by including it as an item at your regular meetings.

Regular and open communication

Such communication among the project team is crucial. It is useful at the start to develop a detailed calendar of meetings for a semester and also to plan some key dates for the year. Team meetings need to take place quite frequently so that you don't lose track of what is happening in the project. The more complex the work, the more frequently they need to be held. In addition to regular meetings of the whole team (if it consists of more than one main researcher with assistance), there need to be more frequent regular meetings between any contract researchers and the researcher they are working with. Such meetings may need to take place as often as once a week or once a fortnight – fieldwork permitting. Your more regular meetings will involve lots of routine project management activities and of necessity will include regular budget updates but should also include progress reports and recurring discussions of the research itself, perhaps based on the progress reports. You might also have your research assistant do a regular email communication bulletin. Set these dates early and in stone. Under no circumstances keep altering them because others want you to. You research must take high priority. Try to include some project team retreats so that you can go away together and enjoy some serious project thinking time. You might use this time to discuss your data or your reading or to workshop your papers.

Dealing with different working styles

Among team members working styles vary. Some members may need huge lead times, for instance, while others may work best under the pressure of fierce deadlines. Try to get to know the different ways of working among team members and accommodate them in your plans. On the other hand, though, because it is a team, you may need to modify your ways in order to progress the team's plans. It's a fine line, but being aware of the issues is a good start.

Time-lines

Your time-lines were produced as part of the project application and revised in line with the reduced budget. They may also need to be revised owing to other things that delay you: achieving ethics approval or getting access to the field, for instance. Clearly your time-line is a moving feast to some extent but it should not be too movable or you will not complete the project on time and it will haunt you while you are trying to do later projects. If some things delay you in one aspect of the project, do other project-related work. This might include such activities as your reading on theory or methods, updating the literature review, working though some thorny conceptual problems or designing research instruments. *There is no such thing as down time on research projects.*

Don't get interrupted by anything outside the project

If you have taken our advice about planning the rest of your teaching and admin work alongside your research, you have no excuses. But some people lack self-discipline. In a highly Pavlovian manner, they respond to every stimulus out there. It is one thing to respond to a reasonable request from your head of school, say, for you to take on some unexpected new activity above and beyond what you knew to expect when you planned your research project's timetable. It is entirely another for you to rush off to everything that looks interesting at the expense of the project which is supposed to be one of your primary responsibilities. If you do this it shows little respect for your research team and also of course drives them crazy. 'No' must be in your vocabulary, and remember, opportunities come along all the time; to miss one is not to miss them all for ever.

Dissemination activities

You should try to keep to your publishing plan but it should be sufficiently flexible to admit out-of-left-field opportunities. However you organise authorship, you should certainly do conference symposia and other public fora together as well as separately. This is vital for the visibility of the project as a whole and it offers you opportunities to collectively test out your ideas in public and to get feedback. It has other benefits, not the least being that you get to go away together and have fun. More invitations to present again on the project are among the usual benefits, unless of course your symposium goes down like a lead balloon. If that happens at least you are there to support each other and can go off together and do group therapeutic activity. We have found that if the papers are badly received the fact itself can provoke some quite generative discussions both at the conference and later. So don't be too gloomy about it. You should make sure you encourage each other to turn conference presentations into papers for peer-refereed journals. Don't make the common mistake of too many conference presentations and not enough publications.

Your dissemination plan may also include developing (and regularly updating!) your website, regular media releases, workshops for industry, promo talks to potential users, talk-back radio and the like. Keep a list of journalists you have found helpful and competent and use them regularly. You do not have to wait till you have conclusive findings; work in progress material is always of interest. Your dissemination plan may also include conferences or workshops that you organise yourselves. These might be highly specialised, by invitation and include only academics in your field. Or they may be designed to speak to policy makers or practitioners and be open to all comers, or specified cohorts. In allocating dissemination responsibilities you might put certain members in charge of overseeing such activities and making sure they happen. It is too easy to let such things slip to the bottom of the list. All research projects should have some sort of *public profile* and you have to build it. In doing so you may take advice from your university's media and PR people. Often the media people are looking for copy and will run stories for you. You should also make sure you and your project are listed on the university's register of expertise or the equivalent.

Acknowledgement

Acknowledging each other's contribution to the work of the team is important. But how does the team recognise and deal with the big ideas of individuals? If someone has had an idea that you can clearly identify as having influenced your thinking it must be acknowledged. However, often in project teams such big ideas are a result of the synergies among the group and it is hard to pin them down to one individual or moment. We thus urge you not to be too precious about this with regard to ideas you think are yours. They may have arisen from the springboard of the group and you may not be acknowledging it sufficiently. On the other hand breakthough thoughts or compelling or evocative new concepts may well deserve to be acknowledged. A little generosity goes a long way. And remember that you need to go on acknowledging the collaboration of your team long after the actual project has ended, whenever you use data collected during the project or the big ideas from it.

Different opportunities among the team

Dealing with these differences is crucial. In many teams there are people who get more invitations than others to strut their stuff at conferences, in print or to the media. If you are such a person try to share some of the opportunities with other members of the team. If you don't, public perceptions of the project will be skewed towards you and also, eventually, there will be undercurrents of resentment within the project team. On the other hand, if you are not one of these people it does you no good to get resentful or envious. Take the opportunities that are available to you to get out and about even if they do not arise from invitations. Volunteer papers, submit proposals for symposia, let people know who you are and of your availability to talk on the project. All such things will enhance your profile in regard to the project and also the project itself – which is the main game, is it not?

Slackers and what to do about them

What do you do if some team members do not share the load equally? One always hopes that if one pulls one's own weight others will pull theirs. But sadly this is not always the case. Sometimes people fall in a heap for personal and entirely understandable reasons, and you can usually live with that for a while as they will eventually come out of it, hopefully sooner rather than later. If it goes on for too long you do need to deal with it, because maybe they can't. However, some people are just plain lazy and are happy for others to do their leg work, and yet others are too busy doing other things to attend properly to the project. It is very hard to sort out such situations. Yet failure to do so can lead to serious rifts within the team. If you have done many of the things we suggest above you may minimise the problem but some people have very thick skins.

Our view is that you should, as always, try to nip the problem in the bud and put the issue up front and on the agenda of meetings. Sometimes all your best efforts have no effect. What do you do then? We think you should cut your losses and count them out. It is not appropriate for them to get credit where credit is not due – and credit for work on your project which they are not actually doing might include some significant benefits to them, such as a reduced work load, access to project money, recognition with regard to project outcomes and so on. That would be plain unfair. You may want to formally negotiate their departure from the project and have funding authorities and the university record the fact. Such a step is serious, and even the threat of it may get them moving. If you do not wish to go that far then we suggest you rewrite the rules the project has negotiated in such a way as to ensure that the person is excluded from project benefits. Certainly their name should not go on any publications or acknowledgements. If, however, they made a big contribution in the early stages of the project and fell by the wayside later, you must acknowledge their early contribution.

Falling out with members of the team

This is not uncommon and neither is it the end of the world, even though it hurts. This can happen at any stage of the project and over any of its activities. Rightly or wrongly, people may feel marginalised in the team or undervalued, they may feel their ideas are neglected, that they carry too much of the load or that some people get more credit than they do. There may be genuine theoretical, methodological or political differences in the team that cannot be reconciled, or totally incompatible working styles. You do need to be alert to the falling-out warning signs in yourself and in others. You might, for example, find yourself constantly anxious or negative about the project, or that after meetings or field trips you come away with feelings of irritability, hostility or disappointment with regard to your co-researchers, or you might feel jealous each time they speak because they are so articulate in comparison with your view of yourself or they get the attention you crave or feel you deserve. All this might lead you to withdraw from them or to make bitchy remarks behind their backs or whatever. In others, these warning signs might include negative body language, withdrawal, hostile, defensive, sarcastic or disruptive behaviour in meetings, a tense and fraught aura when the team is together, the formation of team sub-sets who go their own way or who respond negatively to everything that others do.

How do you deal with such things? You probably need to develop some 'emotional literacy' with regard to your own negative feelings and behaviours. They may arise because you are tired and overworked, because other things are going badly in your life or because you are insecure or paranoid. It is not fair on your co-researchers to project it all on to them. So you do have to get a grip; try to deal with the root causes, get counselling if it will help. On the other hand there may be good reasons for your negative mind set, although if you are paranoid you will be unable to distinguish between these good reasons and your paranoid fantasies. The team may indeed not be working as well as it might. This is the point at which you have to speak up, without dumping on your colleagues, let people know how you feel and ask how the group might collectively improve the situation. This may work; it may not. Some things are not resolvable. Having tried your best you may just have to work and live the project out, or cut your losses and get out if you can do so without too much damage to your reputation or the team. You must then resolve not to work with certain people again.

Four overarching principles apply to the personal dynamics of working in research teams:

- Be very careful who you get into bed with.
- If you are going to err, it's better to err on the side of generosity. There is no place in research for the small-minded or the mean spirited.
- Don't take everything too much to heart – save your angst for the big things that really matter. There is no place in research for the over-sensitive ego.

- If you get seriously, badly, deeply stung don't work with those people again but also don't go around publicly ruining their reputations. They will do that by themselves – eventually, hopefully.

Everybody (or nearly everybody) has a *dream team* in their head. In this team, the ideas would flow, the work would go smoothly, everyone would agree, stimulate and support everyone else all the time, no-one would suffer any angst over the project, everything would run to time and the outputs would be outstanding. Unfortunately, such a dream team doesn't exist. In practice, as with all other relationships, teams need to be worked at. You should no more expect to be part of a perfect team than you expect to have a perfect relationship at all times with your mother, lover or friends. What matters is that the team is good enough and that members of it are prepared to work at making things work.

Relationships between the team and the funder

These are on-going. They don't end once you have the money in your hot little hand (the university's account, actually). All sorts of to-ing and fro-ing will be required, some of which we have already mentioned and is to do with regular reporting and delivery requirements and which may involve dealing with a management team. However, other things may arise as the project proceeds. It is helpful to know that funders often have one person who is your contact and whom you should cultivate. Being on the good side of this person can be very handy at times. Your project might be wise to specify the team member who will be in regular touch with the funder. If there's someone in the team who is particularly adept at that sort of thing, then let him or her deal with it, although you may want to learn some skills from them for future application in different projects. You should always let the funder know if you are seriously behind, or having major difficulties, or have to make significant changes. This is not just a courtesy, it is a necessity. You need to cover yourself and have their agreement to such changes (preferably in writing if need be). But you may also be able to get some help and advice from them with regard to the trouble you are having. The funder is not an ogre, at least not often, and they want to get the project done, and done well, as much as you do. So don't put your funder in an awkward position, ever. It may come back to bite you. Good relationships are always of benefit, personally and professionally. If you are working in a sensitive area and you have some trouble brewing (e.g. hostile journalists phoning you) then make sure you contact the funder, who may have better resources and press officers to deal with it than you have at your disposal. Discuss how best to address the issues.

While funders are not ogres, they can also be pretty damn demanding and can try to squeeze more work out of you than you have been paid for. This may happen at the end of the project in negotiating the final product, or after the project is over they may want you to be involved in a raft of dissemination activities above and beyond those you agreed to. If so, you naturally expect to be paid. Your time requires their money. Don't be a sucker and don't forever give your time for free. They will not respect you in the morning.

Being a member of a team that includes industry partners or government

Many of the things we said above about research teams apply here, but there are some additional matters to consider. These vary for many reasons, including how the funding has been gained. You and your industry partner may have joined forces to gain money from a third party, or perhaps industry has provided the money and contracted you to do the work along with its research staff. There are other options we could list but the point is that the method of funding will determine the power relations within the team and the main pressures on the team. If industry funded you or if it has put more resources into the project than you then it holds most of the aces.

You may find that you and your industry partner have somewhat different values and cultures. Of course you must not assume significant differences exist or go into the research with your mind full of stereotypes – but you may, nonetheless, find such differences and you have to work to try to bridge them. This does not mean that you have to subordinate your culture to theirs, or they theirs to yours. But it probably does mean acknowledging that such differences exist and considering where they advantage the project and where they get in the way. Keep in mind that differences can be very generative and exciting, so don't be afraid of them or dig your heels in unnecessarily.

You will be able to iron out any potentially debilitating differences in the probably protracted process of putting the grant application together – a process that requires both you and your partners to compromise. Such differences may have to do with the research focus or styles or IP and publishing and you may well have found each other's processes annoying. Obviously you would not be proceeding with the research had you not been able to resolve those differences – but that may only have been on the surface and they may simmer for some time. As always, there are no hard-and-fast rules about how to deal with them. The best advice we can offer is to do so early and in as dialogical a manner as is possible.

Winding up, gearing up?

All good things come to an end (and so, thankfully, do the less good). But when is the project finished? Apart from deadlines bearing down on you, there is also the matter of the money running out – and, inevitably, you've so much more that you could still do in relation to the project. Hopefully by this point you will have fulfilled all your promises. You have now:

- Let all your research staff go after due farewells and assistance with future employment.
- Offered your final acknowledgements to participants and undertaken any acts of reciprocity that you deemed necessary and that they wanted.
- Written the final reports.
- Put out the requisite publications, which are being well reviewed and cited.
- Had the impact you hoped.
- Run your budget dry but not overspent it.
- Carefully archived all the material on CDs and in archive boxes or files.

Is that all there is? Is it the end? Well, no, not if you are a career researcher. This is the start of another project. Where you have left off is a place to begin again.

Further Reading

Gitlin, L.N., and Lyons, K. (1996) *Successful Grant Writing: Strategies for Health and Human Service Professionals*, New York: Springer. Aimed primarily at health professionals and academics, this guide is also useful for early career academics and those more advanced, in most disciplines. It is relevant for applications to government, foundations and corporations and takes the reader from a desire to attain research funds to life just after the proposal submission. This advice is complemented by persuasive examples that flesh out the advice. The book covers the following areas: becoming familiar with funding sources; developing your ideas for funding; technical strategies for effective proposal writing; preparing a budget; models of individual and collaborative proposal development and understanding the review process.

Locke, L., Spirduso, W. and Silverman, S. (2000) *Proposals that Work: Guide for Planning Dissertations and Grant Proposals*, Thousand Oaks CA: Sage. This book has three main sections: developing a research proposal for either graduate dissertation or postdoctoral grant applications, finding funds for research proposals and sample proposals. Information in the first section concerns areas of research ethics, developing a rationale as well as being a style guide for writing proposals. In the second section the book contains brief but pertinent advice on finding the right funding source (including advice on cultivating links with industry) advice on planning, budgets and the use of support services. The third section is perhaps the most useful, where all preceding advice is applied in the form of an on-going critical commentary to four actual grant applications.

Orlich, D. (1996) *Designing Successful Grant Proposals*, Alexandria VA: ASCD. Orlich argues that there are three key steps to successful grant proposals: start with a good idea; locate a source that has already funded similar ideas; develop your idea into a well crafted statement. The book is aimed at those attempting to win grants as individuals or as university-based researchers. It covers grants from governments, foundations and industry. It is applicable to any discipline, although much of the advice is particularly pertinent to the social sciences. This book is a straightforward generic guide which supplies practical checklists for each stage of the grant development process. Contains annotated list of resources for grant seekers.

Orosz, J. (2000) *The Insider's Guide to Grant Making: How Foundations Find, Fund, and Manage Effective Programs*, San Francisco: Jossey Bass. Although this book is aimed primarily at new workers in foundations, it is also an informative 'insider' view for grant seekers. As the author points out, all roads in philanthropy lead to the programme officer, and, this book could be a valuable part of a grant seeker's research into the culture of foundations and the professional life of the officer they deal with. The book focuses on US private foundations but most of the practices outlined are also applicable to community and corporate foundations. The author argues that charitable and philanthropic foundations operate (ideally) as an instrument for transforming private funds into public benefit, a process that has been on-going since Plato's academy. Foundations concentrate on philanthropy (root causes) as opposed to charity (meeting immediate needs), and innovation instead of on-going programmes, and so are well placed for the early career researcher. The book includes an extensive bibliography of foundations.

Ries, J. and Leukefeld, C. (1995) *Applying for Research Funding: Getting Started and Getting Funded,* Thousand Oaks CA: Sage. An accessible and useful guide to developing a research proposal and managing the time it takes to complete it. The authors argue that success in grant applications is achieved through attention to three key areas: focused research, networking, personal and management skills. The book develops strategies for each of these areas. Emphasis is given to developing 'inventories' of personal and professional strengths. These assist in knowing whether you need to collaborate with other researchers or strengthen certain areas yourself. Comprehensive definitions of types of grants, contracts, as well as government and non-government funding bodies are offered. Other topics include how to write a persuasive application, how to target the application for the reviewers and reacting to the reviewers' decision. Most of the information can be used by researchers in any disciplines, although the book draws on examples from the sciences.

Schumacher, D. (1992) *Get Funded! A Practical Guide for Scholars seeking Research Support from Business*, Newbury Park CA: Sage. Although this book is aimed at researchers who are advanced in their careers, it contains useful advice for early career researchers in an environment where industry partnerships are important to research funding. Much of the advice could best be utilised if the early career researcher worked in collaboration with more experienced researchers. The main argument is that successful applications depend on developing and maintaining good relations with industry personnel. Successful applications depend on good relations as much as on the quality of the proposal itself. Researchers must discover what the company needs are. Developing networks within industry is the best way to do this. Researchers need to develop an understanding of business culture and the ability to communicate effectively using the dominant codes of that culture. Successful applications offer industry an opportunity for collaboration that can benefit the enterprise. Schumacher argues that industry needs to be treated as a valued partner that has genuine interests in contributing to all aspects and directions of the research. The corporate perspective about research is informed by relevant interviews with industry, and the university perspective is informed by debates around the role of universities and the ethics of industry linkage.

Websites

This is a selection of the many websites available. Remember that nearly all large charitable foundations which fund research are likely to have websites and you can find them using your Internet search engine.

Australian Research Council (ARC), http://www.arc.gov.au/. The main body that administers funding for researchers working at Australian universities. This site provides information about the ARC, its Competitive Research programmes, grant application information and previously funded research projects.

British Academy http://britac3.britac.ac.uk/index.html. This site offers information concerning grants in the humanities and social sciences. Grants are available to support advanced research at postdoctoral level (or equivalent). Grants are offered for the support of scholars who are normally resident in the UK, except the programmes for visiting scholars. The Academy sponsors approximately forty major research projects (called Academy Research Projects), each organised and run by its own committee. These projects aim to make available fundamental research tools of benefit to a wide range of scholars. The website also contains contact details for those wishing to pursue country-specific agreements for individual research visits and joint projects.

Catalogue of Federal Domestic Assistance, [USA] http://www.cfda.gov/public/browse_typast.asp?catcode=B. Described by Orlich *Designing Successful Grant Proposals* (1996) as the most important index for identifying federal resources. Lists specific project grants, which can include fellowships, scholarships, research grants, training grants, traineeships and experimental and demonstration grants. The CFDA website is updated twice yearly at approximately the same time as the printed *Catalogue of Federal Domestic Assistance* is published (June and December).

Economic and Social Research Council (ESRC), [UK] http://www.esrc.ac. uk/index.asp. Describes itself as 'the UK's leading research funding and training agency addressing economic and social concerns'. Contains current list of all research activities where applications are invited, with links to further information, application forms and thematic research priorities. It also provides links to commissioning updates, and flags possible future funding opportunities. Also contains searchable database of research projects funded, their duration and the amount funded.

EU Grants, http://europa.eu.int/comm/secretariat_general/sgc/aides/index_en.htm. Contains information relating to EU funding for research. Funding. encourages collaboration between member nations of the European Union as well as international research collaborations. The focus of calls for research is on science and technology but there is scope for social science projects. The site has links to current calls for research, the EU research archive and a list of names to contact for further information.

Foundation Center, [USA] http://fdncenter.org/research/. This contains extensive information on private and public philanthropic foundations in the US. Searches can be made for basic information of more than 70,000 private and community foundations in the US. Searches can also be made of annotated links to private foundations by subject or geographic keyword. Includes list of the 100 largest US grant-making foundations ranked by total giving. Includes on-line tutorials 'Proposal Budgeting Basics' and 'Proposal Writing Short Course'. Includes information on trends in grant expenditure.

Foundation for Research, Science and Technology (FRST), [New Zealand], http://www.frst.govt.nz/index.cfm. The foundation invests in research, science and technology (RS&T) on behalf of the New Zealand government. It funds research in areas such as social, economic and public life in New Zealand and research in innovation-based enterprises and their associated consequences. The site includes information on research tenders for private companies in areas such as information and communication technology.

Funders Online, [Europe], http://www.fundersonline.org/about/. Funders Online facilitates access to online funding information on foundations and corporate funders active in Europe. Information and tips on how to research independent funders, how to package your project proposal and where to find additional information, both in print and on-line, on foundations and corporate funders.

Grants Information Center, [USA], http://www.library.wisc.edu/libraries/Memorial/ grants/proposal.htm. There are many sites that provide proposal writing advice. This site addresses a US audience but may be useful to other grant seekers. It includes advice on letters of enquiry and has sample proposals and covers proposal writing for industry, government, private and public foundations. It also provides a list of websites for proposal writing. Site of the Grants Information Center, University of Wisconsin – Madison.

Intellectual Property, http://www.magna.com.au/~prfbrown/ip_links.html. A comprehensive resource site for IP-related information. It includes searches relevant to Australia, New Zealand, the United States, Canada, Europe, Japan, Spain and the Philippines.

Illinois Researcher Information Service (IRIS), [USA], http://gateway.library. uiuc.edu/iris/. IRIS is a unit of the University of Illinois Library at Urbana– Champaign. IRIS offers three web-based funding and research services: the IRIS Database of federal and private funding opportunities in all disciplines; the IRIS Alert Service; and the IRIS Expertise Service. The IRIS Database contains over 8,000 active federal and private funding opportunities in the sciences, social sciences, arts and humanities. Users can search IRIS by sponsor, deadline date, key word and other criteria. Most IRIS records contain live links to sponsor websites, electronic forms, or Electronic Research Administration (ERA) portals. The IRIS Database is updated daily. Researchers at subscribing institutions can create their own IRIS search profiles and detailed electronic CVs ('biosketches') and post them to a web-accessible database for viewing by colleagues at other institutions, programme officers at federal and private funding agencies, and private companies.

Marsden Fund, [New Zealand], http://www.rsnz.govt.nz/funding/marsden_fund/ #Marsden. This fund invests in investigator-initiated research aimed at exploring the 'frontiers of new knowledge'. The research is 'not subject to government's socio-economic priorities'. The Marsden Fund is operated as a fully contestable fund. Eligibility to bid to the fund is unrestricted provided that the research proposed is either to be carried out in New Zealand or, if its nature demands that it be carried out elsewhere, by New Zealand-based researchers. Funds are allocated for the support of research projects or programmes, or for the support of individual researchers, including postdoctoral fellows. The fund supports research in the sciences, the social sciences and the humanities.

National Research Foundation (NRF), [South Africa], http://www.nrf.ac.za/. The South African government's national agency responsible for promoting and supporting basic and applied research as well as 'innovation'. Provides grant information for the humanities, social and natural sciences, engineering and technology; including indigenous knowledge.

World Bank, http://web.worldbank.org/WBSITE/EXTERNAL/OPPORTUNI-TIES/0,,pagePK:95647~theSitePK:95480,00.html. This site offers information on grants and consulting that may be useful to early career researchers whose work is related to the goals of development assistance. A limited number of grants are available through the bank, either funded directly or managed through partnerships. Most are designed to encourage innovation, collaboration with other organizations, and participation by stakeholders at national and local levels. The bank regularly uses a variety of consulting services from individuals and firms at the headquarters or in country offices. The bank also offers research internships (unpaid) for graduate students to gain experience in an international environment on development issues.

Index